Defining Creativity
The Art and Science of Great Ideas

Wouter Boon

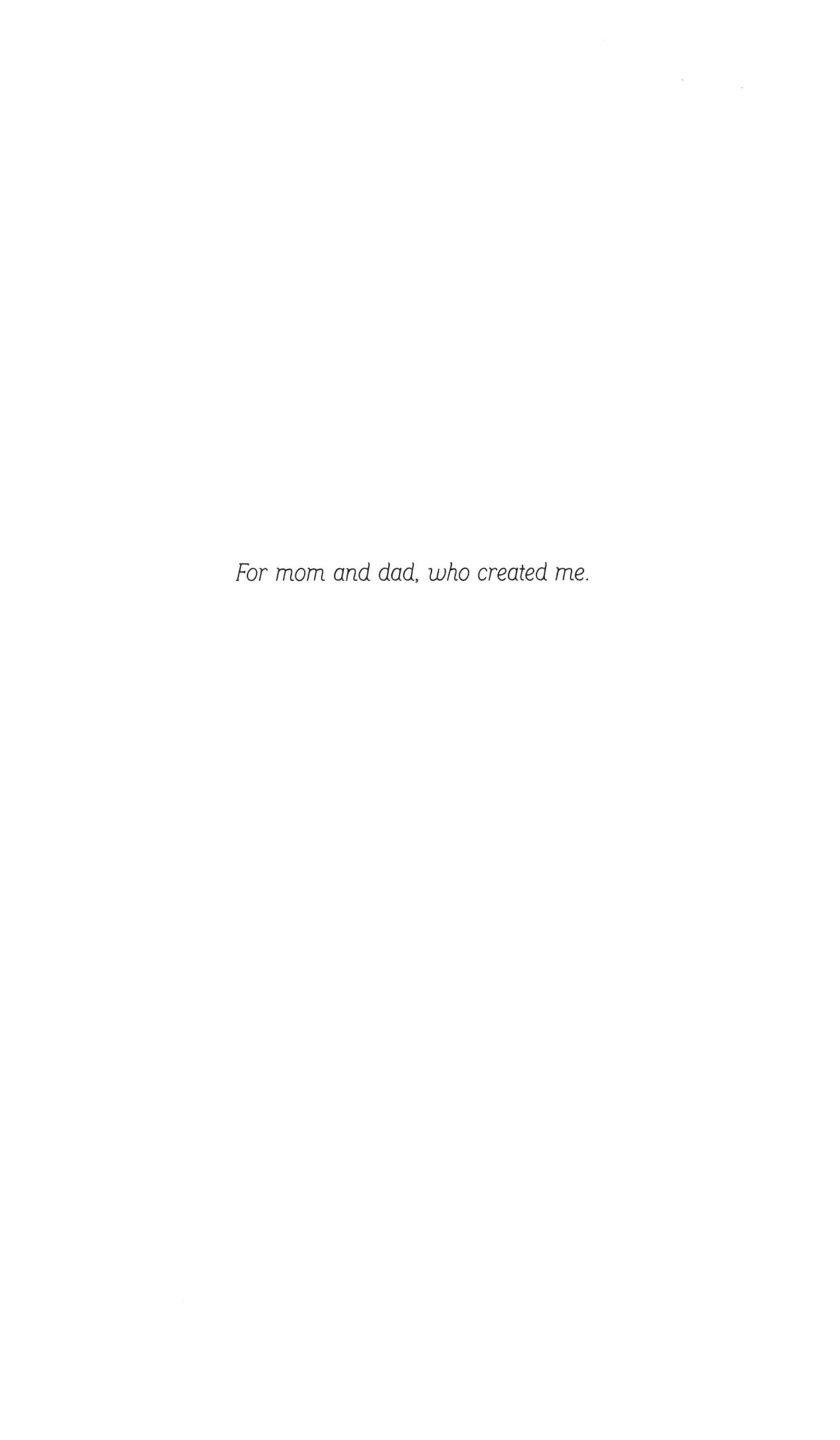

For mom and dad, who created me.

Colophon

BIS Publishers
Building Het Sieraad
Postjesweg 1, 1057 DT Amsterdam
The Netherlands
T +31 (0)20 515 02 30
bis@bispublishers.nl
www.bispublishers.nl

Text: Wouter Boon
Design: Rick de Zwart and Hans van der Baan
ISBN 978 90 6369 345 9
Copyright © 2014 Wouter Boon and BIS Publishers.
www.definingcreativity.com

Wouter Boon

Defining Creativity

The Art and Science of Great Ideas

BIS

Contents

 Contents

Introduction

Omnipresent

Creativity has become a buzz word over the past decades. Most of us want to be called creative – even companies and governments. The reason is that creativity represents a special ability and thus gives us a certain status. But it's not just that. Creativity is extremely handy. It is an invisible tool for making stuff, solving problems, and innovation. And it's not just practical; it is also a form of self-expression and experienced as enjoyable. For all these different reasons artists, inventors, and scientists fruitfully use it to create works of art, products, and theories. Creativity, however, is not just reserved for a creative elite, but also constantly used in everyday life by people who are generally not regarded as creative. It is thus used by everyone and omnipresent in the world around us.

Illusive

Nevertheless, most people regard the concept of creativity as difficult to grasp. Even scientists have a hard time formulating the 'laws of creativity.' One of the reasons for this is that not all output of creativity is necessarily regarded as 'creative.' And that's because there is a difference between being personally creative, which means that you simply create something that you've never created before, and creating something historical, because it changes the way people view the world. In the latter meaning, something is only regarded creative when the experts in a domain judge it a valuable addition to the domain, which turns creativity into a label attached to certain ideas, and thus a subjective, cultural and dynamic construct.

Another reason why creativity is not really an exact science is that it's not ruled by one single mental process or personality trait; we use different parts of our brain and different personalities to be creative. For example, creative minds are known for being autonomous – even egocentric – while at the same time it is important that they interact socially in order to learn from others or convince them of the greatness of an idea. What makes creativity even more complicated is that different creative domains require different cognitive skills. Inventing a rocket is obviously not the same as painting on a canvas. And making a film is not the same as composing music.

Creativity is also illusive, because we still don't know exactly what happens in our brain when we are being creative. Which is why it is hard to measure someone's creativity. There are psychological tests on creative potential, but their predictive capacity is only limited. And even if we know that we are creative – because everyone tells us so – we can't simply evoke it whenever

 Introduction

we want. Sometimes, when we are looking hard for it we cannot find it. Then, when we lay the creative project aside, the creativity suddenly comes to us in the form of an 'aha' moment. But although creativity is subjective, complex, and illusive it is definitely not indefinable.

Comprehensive

Defining Creativity explains the meaning of creativity in a comprehensive manner. It covers the most important aspects of creativity – sourced from a wide variety of established books – and approaches the theme from completely different perspectives, such as from a philosophical, historical, cultural, psychological, biological, and even evolutionary viewpoint. To prevent the book from becoming too theoretical, it explains the different angles by describing the ideas, behaviour, and works of some of the most historic artistic, inventive, and scientific minds. In a way this book is therefore also a tribute to the most well-known creative minds, such as Charles Darwin, Vincent van Gogh, and Steve Jobs. Their works, and that of many other geniuses, are still enjoyed and admired today. Not just the ones that tickle our senses, such as films, books, songs, and paintings, but also those that have innovated our world and help us to adapt to changing environments. It is on these great ideas that we've built our entire world and will keep building our world in the future ahead.

1.

Building Life

If I had to define life in a word,
it would be life is creation

Claude Bernard

Bringing into existence

The standard definition of creativity that you will find in a dictionary is something along the lines of *"The ability to bring something into existence."* If we go by this definition, acts of creativity are not exclusively reserved for human beings, but can also be attributed to nature's creations. The very first natural act of creation – as far as modern science knows – is the *Big Bang.* This huge explosion created our universe some 13.8 billion years ago. Subsequently it created planet earth, about 4.5 billion years ago, and eventually us, the modern *Homo sapiens*, roughly two hundred thousand years ago. The Christian equivalent of the Big Bang, God, had a similar act of creation. The Christian Bible's first sentence even literally describes it: *"In the beginning God created the Heaven and the Earth."* What both acts of creation have in common with human creativity is that they created something new. This is the first important attribute that makes something creative; bringing something into existence that is entirely new.

Building blocks

There is one important difference between the scientific and the Christian conception of our world; the Big Bang used existing building blocks to create the universe, while God created something out of nothing. You might be inclined to think that the Big Bang also created the universe out of nothing, since we don't know exactly what was there before the Big Bang. However, scientist generally agree that our universe was made out of *something*. It was extremely tiny – about 1 billionth of the size of an atom – but it was something. Greek scholars 2,000 years ago already philosophised about creation *ex nihilo* – out of nothing. They reasoned that this couldn't be possible, and that whatever created the universe should share nature's properties. In other words, creating out of nothing is as possible as conjuring a rabbit from an empty hat. Everything created in our universe, human creations included, is built with existing building blocks. There is even a continuum between natural and man-made creations; from the very first brainless prebiotic reactions on this planet to human beings being able to intelligently create physical objects.

Let's start with prebiotic chemistry creating the very first building blocks. When earth was still an extremely unfriendly environment for human beings to live on, a handful of basic molecules, such as ammonia, methane, water, and carbon dioxide, combined into new forms by simply reacting with each other – sometimes aided by a bolt of lightning. Methane and oxygen, for example, could react to form formaldehyde and water. Four billion years ago only a very limited amount of reactions were possible. Then, after many combinations, the first step to building an actual living organism was the creation of a cell. Proteins could form the membranes that served as the boundary of a cell. Once sugar molecules combined into nucleic acids, DNA could be composed, the building block essential for creating human beings.

Intelligent life

When DNA-based life made its entrance, it was constantly steered into new directions. This was possible because DNA is susceptible to error, which leads to mutations in the code and creates differences within a species. As the naturalist Charles Darwin described in his famous evolution theory, these differences can be an advantage in the struggle for survival in an environment that constantly changes due to climate changes, exploding volcanoes, and meteor impacts. According to Darwin's theory those that survive pass on their advantageous traits to their offspring, thus slowly changing their species. This is also how, relatively recently, fish started to walk on land, which turned them into mammals; mammals started to climb into trees, which turned them into apes; and apes climbed out of the trees again, which turned them into human beings – in the shortest summary possible. The latter step was a radical one, since almost suddenly life turned much more intelligent.

The first intelligent acts of creation came from *Homo erectus* ('upright man'), our direct ancestor. Even though the brain of Homo erectus 1.5 million years ago resembled that of a human baby, with its opposable thumbs it was able to turn a stone into a tool by shaping it with another stone into a hand axe. In a way, this was the very first piece of technology. Once Homo erectus became skilful at shaping these stones, they were made in their thousands, not just as tools, but also because our ancestor enjoyed making them for aesthetic reasons – and maybe even to show off skill. These stones can therefore also be seen as the first pieces of art. Once Homo erectus knew how to make tools and weapons, it was able to kill bigger animals, form bigger social groups, and learn how to set up camps and fires, allowing its brain to grow steadily. In no time – in the light of the existence of planet earth, of course – hominoids became extremely ingenious and productive. If you look at the complete continuum between natural and human creations, we've become quite advanced. While four billion years ago a carbon atom could only form a few hundred configurations, today we can use that same carbon atom to build anything we can imagine, from a virus to a skyscraper.

The thing that makes human creation special compared to natural creation is that we create consciously and are not solely directed by external, physical and chemical forces. And we're not indifferent about it; we actually enjoy being creative. Which is why today we continuously bring a wide variety of things into existence; art, stories, theories, performances, computer programs, tools, buildings, and so on. And, as mentioned earlier, we always use existing building blocks.

A classic example of an invention made with building blocks, is the printing press. Around 1440, Johannes Gutenberg, a goldsmith and entrepreneur living in the famous German wine region Rhineland, started tinkering with a wine press. Gutenberg was not particularly interested in wine, though; he was more interested in words and used the essential part of the wine press, the screw mechanism, to create a printing press. The building blocks he used already existed for hundreds and even thousands of years; the ink, the paper, the movable type, and the key element, the wine press itself. The printing press, however, was truly groundbreaking; it radically changed the creative domain of books, because they could now easily be multiplied. What the internet only very recently did for the explosion of content generation and distribution, the printing press did for the reproduction of books – and, directly following this invention, the Bible in particular.

The Creation of Adam

Clearly, the printing press was something entirely new. In art, however, novelty is not always as easy to establish. Works of art often look quite similar – especially for a layman. A work that has succeeded in making a lasting impression, even though depicting an in itself well-known biblical scene, is *The Creation of Adam*. This fresco, commissioned by Pope Julius II at the beginning of the 16th century, was painted by Michelangelo Buonarroti on the ceiling of the Sistine Chapel in Rome. It was part of a total of nine scenes from the *Book of Genesis* and displays a grey-bearded God that is about to transfer the spark of life to Adam by reaching out to touch his finger. This in itself was not unique. It was not uncommon for the Vatican to commission someone to paint a scene from the Bible, and the scene of Adam being brought to life by the hand of God had certainly been painted before. So, why did it become so famous? There are several reasons. Any artistic project initiated by the Pope would receive more attention than usual – after all, he is as close to God as one can get. Especially when painted in one of the most important buildings of the Vatican; the house where popes are elected. The Creation of Adam was also part of a work unique for its size; the complete fresco measures 1,100 m² and took Michelangelo from 1508 until 1512 to complete. Another factor that helped make this creation so well-known is the importance of Italy and the Renaissance in the history of art. Italy at that time was the centre of the creative world. Being in the right place, at the right time also proved important for the attention The Creation of Adam received. All these factors made the work special enough to stand out.

However, what made this work truly unique in the domain of Renaissance art was that Michelangelo depicted the creation of Adam in a completely new way. First of all, Michelangelo was very advanced at creating anatomically correct bodies. By depicting Adam fully naked, resembling a real human being rather than something created with a brush, he was given a soul, as it were, which made the scene extremely convincing. At the same time, making the outstretched hand of God the centre and focus of the entire image in such an elegant manner turned God into an omnipotent being that was clearly able to create with the ease of a simple gesture. Fashioning the mystery of divine creation in such a realistic form made the work entirely new and thus creative.

Imagination

Similar to those of Gutenberg's, the building blocks for Michelangelo's work can easily be summed up as; he used brushes and paint. But there are, of course, more building blocks than that. You could say that all the knowledge he possessed, such as his knowledge of the Sistine Chapel, the Vatican, the Bible, Christianity, but also of the human body, formed the intellectual input for his creation. When talking about building blocks, you might be inclined to think of physical building blocks, such as the literal bricks, metal, and glass that create architectural works. However, what is unique about human creativity is that we don't just play around with bricks, but always start the creative process with knowledge we've obtained through learning and past experiences.

Thanks to our imagination, we are able to create ideas in our minds that are based on this knowledge – before we actually start building anything physical. What our imagination basically does is it takes different pieces of knowledge from our memory and compiles them into something new. More precisely, imagination creates an actual image in our mind, using the same part of our brain that is used for seeing. When we *normally* see something, our brain transforms the images from the outside world that are caught on our retina into neural signals. Subsequently, our perception interprets these signals by categorising them. When you see a perfectly round object, for example, your brain will categorise it as 'ball.' When it's yellow and not too big, it will categorise it as what it most likely is; a tennis ball. When we use our imagination, however, our brain follows the opposite neural pathway; it first categorises something in a new way and then turns it into an image.

An example of an idea created by imagination is the world-famous *Sydney Opera House* designed by the Dane Jørn Utzon. The design was submitted by Utzon for a competition, launched by the Australian government of New South Wales. It is said that it was Utzon's love for sailing – an in itself obvious association when you design a building that is located in a harbour – that made him imagine a building resembling sails. He couldn't have used an existing image from his memory, because no one had built such a construction before yet. Therefore, in his mind he will have had to merge the image of the sails – a vivid memory – with that of a building. Without having thought about any of the technical building blocks, he sketched this vision and entered it in the competition. Obviously, the shape was so impressive that the committee chose Utzon's 'ship' out of 233 submissions from 32 countries, before even knowing whether it was possible to physically build it. Much later this proved extremely difficult.

Making visible

An important form of creation that draws from our imagination is discovery. It consists of making visible or known what has already been created by someone or something else, but hasn't been seen before. That's why to discover literally means to uncover. Since what we discover with our imagination is invisible, it's for the most part a theoretical act that happens inside the brain. For instance, take the discovery of our human DNA by James Watson and Francis Crick in 1953. At the time, our genetic code couldn't be observed directly at an atomic level. So, in order to make it visible, Watson and Crick had to build a theoretical structure. Since they hadn't really conducted any previous DNA experiments of their own, they primarily used existing knowledge to form the building blocks for their invention. Rosalind Franklin's X-Ray images and Jerry Donhue's knowledge of hydrogen bonds, for example, were essential building blocks for this discovery. After Watson and Crick had put all their knowledge together and cracked the code of the human DNA, others in turn could build on their discovery. In fact, all of modern genetic engineering is based on this tiny, but hugely important building block.

Regardless of whether the creations in our universe are natural or human, artistic or scientific, physical or theoretical, visible or invisible, they are all created with existing building blocks. And even when we, Homo sapiens, die out, acts of creation will continue to happen. In this book, however, we will only look at *human* acts of creativity that are conscious, directed, and – most importantly – entirely new.

2.

The Value of Originality

*It is better to fail in originality
than to succeed in imitation*

Herman Melville

Appreciation

Apart from novelty, there is another important attribute that helps to define a work as creative; value. Value is not necessarily meant as a monetary expression, but stands for the appreciation that is given to a work, invention, or theory by an audience. Value has different meanings in different creative domains; e.g. it can be musical, literary, or scientific. In the artistic domain value commonly means a pleasure for the senses, while in the domains of invention and science it is associated with usefulness. But regardless of the domain, value is a word most people wouldn't intuitively link to creativity. It even feels as though judging creativity on the basis of its value is contradictory to its intrinsic meaning. After all, most creative minds create from an inner urge to create. They don't generally care what the outside world thinks of it.

However, value is an important part of the definition of creativity. The reason for this is that, in Western society, the term 'creativity' is generally used for works that stand out and make a difference. Not just because they are new, but because they change how we view and interact with the world. If we wouldn't separate the valuable works from the works that are merely new, then creativity would be fairly common; people have novel thoughts and create novel works all the time.

Take dreams, for example. Though dreams can have identical central themes, most dreams are quite unique, using different storylines, different people and objects, and different details. If you would translate these unique dreams into books or films – so that the outside world could have access to them and form an opinion about them – the chance that you would receive appreciation is pretty slim. These stories are new, but they won't be judged as creative. Even if you apply this thought experiment

 Chapter 2

to an established creative domain such as poetry, the result remains the same. When you put words in a random order and call it modern poetry, it's not very likely that people would accept it as a creative work. It would be new, but not valued.

Communicable form

By adding value to the definition of creativity, we don't just add external judgment to creativity, but also separate being *personally* creative from being *historically* creative. On a personal level, we are all creative to some extent. It's not particularly difficult to be personally creative, since this can be as simple as using the available ingredients in your kitchen to cook a meal, finding your way back to your hotel when lost in an unfamiliar city, or making a subtle pun in a conversation. Though these actions use the brain in a creative manner, they will never enter the public arena of creativity because these actions are solely meant for personal use. In other words, the intention of the creative action is not to produce something that will stand out in a certain creative domain. So, to be historically creative, you need to at least have the intention to contribute something to a creative domain.

For an idea to be considered historically creative, it needs to be shared with the world and therefore translated into a communicable form – in jargon referred to as a 'medium' – so that the world has a chance to see or experience it. Only then can it be valued by them. This means that a mad professor who is convinced that he is the first person on earth to have successfully invented a *perpetual mobile* (read: a machine that defies the laws of thermodynamics by producing at least the same amount of energy as it consumes) will never be acknowledged as creative if he keeps his invention to himself and lives like a hermit in a shed that nobody knows of.

Van Gogh

Value is a difficult attribute, because it's not intrinsic to a creative work, but dependent on its audience. This makes creativity a subjective and dynamic concept; sometimes the audience only grants value to a work after the artist has already died. Vincent van Gogh is a good example of someone who hardly earned any public appreciation during his life, whereas today his works are judged quintessentially creative. Van Gogh, born in 1853, was indeed a painter who had a new style of painting; he used colours in unorthodox ways, applied thick layers of paint, and put true emotion into his paintings. All these elements were quite progressive at the end of the 19th century. Still, during his life only a handful of people valued his work. Among them was Gauguin, which is not a surprise since he was a fellow post-impressionist with a similar style of painting. Another important supporter was his brother Theo who was an art dealer in Paris and bought all of Van Gogh's paintings. Unfortunately, though, he wasn't able to sell his younger brother's work. People didn't appreciate Van Gogh's work, because they considered it a little too modern and daring for its time. So when the Dutch painter died at the premature age of 37, his works were not worth very much – some of his studies were sold at the market for 10 cents apiece. However, immediately after Van Gogh's death, art buyers started to discover his work and within a relatively short period of time it became highly prized. Today his works are among the most-valued – and expensive – art pieces in the world.

But creativity isn't only dynamic because the taste of the audience might change over time. The fact that external judgment might even influence the creator also makes creativity a volatile construct. Whether you are a musician or a painter, or even a scientist, when people are visiting your concerts, buying your paintings, or elaborately citing from your scientific articles, you are considered successful. As most people experience success as something comfortable, they might be inclined to please the society that appreciates their work. Some creators might even become a bit lazy and simply perform the same trick over and over again. Thus when some creative minds get used to a 'successful' lifestyle, selling their creative work becomes more important than creating something new. Which then gives value a monetary meaning after all.

Intellectual Property

In Western cultures creative works are often valued when they are considered 'original.' This word refers to being the origin, or very first copy, of something new. Since the majority of people is better at copying than creating something new, only a small percentage of people is truly original. In sociocultural terms originality therefore has intrinsic value; people who make original works are seen as smart and independent thinkers. The value that is incorporated in a creative work is thus reflected on the creator. And that's why some people make an effort to come across as original, even though they don't produce anything new. They merely adopt the status by becoming part of a subculture and by adopting certain looks or engaging in activities that will make them stand out in the crowd. Of course, this is not the same as being creative.

Western society has even institutionalised the importance of originality in intellectual property laws. The very first law to protect a creator's originality was the *Statute of Anne*, a British copyright law enacted in 1710. This law was *"an act for the encouragement of learning"* and granted a copyright that lasted 14 years. The idea behind it was to encourage authors to share their knowledge and not be afraid of others stealing their ideas once they would publish their work. The Statute of Anne was thus implemented to stimulate innovation. Ironically, many of today's intellectual property laws are actually used to thwart innovation, for example by registering patents to rule out competitors or simply to be able to sell the rights. This is why some people are convinced that the laws dealing with originality need to be modernised in a manner that makes it easier to use and improve existing ideas in order to stimulate innovation.

In some cultures intellectual property laws are not taken very seriously. The reason for this is that originality has never entered their domain of creativity. Especially in primitive and collectivist cultures, conceptions of creativity are quite different. Similar to the first pieces of art described in the previous chapter, artworks in most primitive cultures need to represent a perfect version of the original to be given a cultural meaning. For example, think of the ornate masks still used in animist ceremonies or celebrations. The similarity between these artifacts is crucial for continuing the cultural tradition, expressing religion, and being ritually effective. In these cultures craftsmanship is used for creating identical 'art,' not in order to constantly create something new. Therefore creativity in this context is primarily about craftsmanship, not about originality, and thus comes closer to the basic definition of creativity we find in the dictionary; the simple act of creation. Even today, in many modern Asian cultures originality is not necessarily considered a positive attribute, since the group is given more importance than the individual. Standing out as a person won't necessarily give you a special status, as this is often considered offensive. In many ancient and non-Western cultures creativity is thus not about originality or change, but about craftsmanship and continuation.

Imitating nature

The fact that we value originality today in the Western world is not a very old phenomenon. During the Renaissance originality had a different meaning; it meant truth of observation. The artists considered most original were those who were best at imitating nature. The artist simply had the task of conveying what religious and mythical figures should look like. Take Michelangelo's statue of the biblical David, who beat Goliath with a sling. It took Michelangelo from 1501 until 1504 to complete the impressive statue which is over 5 meters tall, almost making us forget that Goliath was the giant. With this statue Michelangelo tried to mimic divine creation. In fact, he believed that the image of David already resided in the block of stone. He was merely making it visible. Though the statue's head and hands are relatively large compared to its slender body, it still looks like a pretty perfect human being today.

In Michelangelo's days making art was also primarily considered a craft. Painters worked as apprentices for a master in a studio and had to learn how to make their own paint and brushes. The most successful apprentices were those who could best imitate their masters. Imitation was a virtue, not a crime, and most contemporary high art, such as classical music and literature, had similar origins. Technical mastery of the tools was more important than creating something unique. However, this started to change by the middle of the 16th century. Instead of painting icons and scenes on large panels in the name of God, commissioned by the church and nobility, individuals started to work alone and paint with oil on canvas. They availed of smaller and more varied commissions, which made them more autonomous and mobile. Due to these developments, artists started to personally sign their work. This enhanced their status and slowly but surely turned them into a prestigious, independent class, distinguishing themselves from the masses. The most successful artists even became celebrities.

Point and shoot

At the end of the 18th century, the Industrial Revolution made working autonomously even more accessible. To stay in the realm of painters; paint, frames, and brushes were mass-produced and could be purchased instead of having to be made by hand in a studio. The tools of creation thus became available to a much wider group of people. Then, at the end of the 20th century, the barrier to entry was lowered once again with the advent of the personal computer; painting now only required the right software. And with the invention of the 3D printer quite recently, we might even enter a new industrial revolution, in which, for example, people can develop and produce their own physical works – without needing an expensive mould maker or factory.

Today we can literally create with the snap of a finger; we imitate nature by simply taking a photo of it with our pocket-sized point-and-shoot cameras that even allow us to directly distribute it online. Which is obviously much easier than having to carry around a huge, technical, and expensive camera, needing access to a dark room, high-quality printer, etc. However, there is one catch to the ease with which we can take photos: it doesn't make us skilled photographers. Or, more generally, it doesn't make us creative. The accessibility of creative tools simply means that we can more easily copy or mimic existing creative works and styles, and thus only allows us to make more of the same. And in our culture more of the same is the opposite of creativity.

Repetitive art

However, once you have reached a certain creative status, creating more of the same doesn't have to be a problem. In the 60s, Andy Warhol even became famous for his repetitive art, which simply copied existing objects and multiplied them, such as the famous cans of *Campbell* soup. With his *Pop art* he negated the importance of talent and touted the fact that anyone could copy his technique. Accordingly, and with a taste for irony, he called his studio *The Factory*. The British artist Damien Hirst, clearly a descendant of Warhol, is also known for copying his – in themselves creative – works many, many times. Of his famous spot paintings, he created 1,365 similar copies. Most of them weren't even produced by him personally, but by his apprentices, which, for that matter, is very similar to the master and his pupils working in a Renaissance studio. Hirst, being one of the richest creative artists alive, demonstrates how ambiguous the meaning of value is in the realm of creativity. The value is not only given to the work itself, but equally so to the creator or even his signature. Another British artist, Robin Gunningham, known as Banksy, proved this point quite well in 2013 by selling his street art through an unknown middleman at a New York street stall for $60 apiece. Since nobody recognised the works as original Banksys, only 7 pieces were sold. The real value per piece was later estimated at $32,000, whereas the almost identical 'fake' Banksys sold throughout London were worthless. This proves that the value of the creator himself today reflects as much on his works, as vice versa.

3.

Cultural Change

A man's mind stretched to a new idea never goes back to its original dimensions

Oliver Wendell Holmes Jr.

Memes

If the value given by an audience to an idea or person is essential for it or him to be regarded as creative, then creativity is a cultural phenomenon. This is why creative and cultural domains show a strong resemblance. A cultural domain is formed by *memes*, which are pieces of information that the members of this culture learn, remember, live by, and pass on to the next generation. Think of languages, values, songs, jokes, recipes, laws, and so on. These memes define the culture and are there to keep it alive. Nevertheless, memes always change, as people introduce new memes. But they are only adopted by a culture if enough people appreciate these individual changes. In the creative domain these individual changes are the new works, inventions, or theories introduced by creative minds. If the audience within the creative domain likes these new ideas, the creative domain changes. Creativity thus lives by an organic set of rules, invented, kept alive and constantly changed by people.

Just like cultures and subcultures, creative domains also come in different sizes. A creative domain can be as big or as small as you wish to define it. 'Mathematics' is a domain, but so is 'algebra'. Or on the artistic side of the spectrum; 'film' is a domain. However, it also contains a smaller domain called 'art-house,' which specifically refers to films with plots that are less popular, made with a smaller budget, and more often with unknown actors. You can make the domain a bit smaller still and call it *Dogme 95*. This domain is an avant-garde filmmaking movement that was founded in 1995 by Danish directors Lars von Trier and Thomas Vinterberg. They wanted to make films based on pure values around story, acting, and theme. More importantly, they wrote a manifesto in which they formulated a list of very specific rules. Thus it became a very well-defined creative domain, explicitly banning the use of external props, technical enhancements, and other artificial additives. What is atypical about Dogme 95 is that the rules of creating art are usually not set in stone. They grow organically over a long period of time and constantly change, just like cultures do.

Gatekeepers

Up and until now, we've discussed how an audience can be the judge of whether an idea is creative or not. But every creative domain actually has a much more specific group that decides whether or not a new idea is valuable enough to change the domain. This group consists of experts, and each domain has its own. Examples of experts are opinion leaders, journalists, scholars, exhibitors, publishers, and investors. What these people have in common is that they know their domain very well, are well-connected inside the domain, and have the authority to convince others of the value of specific ideas. Think of the editors of a scientific journal who decide whether or not to publish an article, the DJ who chooses to play a song on the radio, or the gallery that decides to exhibit a promising artist. This makes the experts the gatekeepers of a domain and an intermediary between the creator and a bigger audience. They thus work as catalysts for ideas to be distributed.

Typically, experts form a select group that know each other well and constantly discusses the value of new ideas. That's why each specific group of experts can be seen as a homogeneous entity – a subculture of its own, as it were – that has internalized the rules and conventions of a domain. If you would ask 10 people, generally interested in art, to assess a new style of art and you ask 10 experts within that domain the same question, the amateur ratings will be all over the map, whereas the experts will be remarkably consistent in their assessment. So, in general, the experts largely have consensus on what is new and valuable and what is not.

In recent years, the gatekeeper's role of the expert has been somewhat democratised thanks to the internet. The reason for this is that it has now become much easier to share content directly with an audience; you don't need a publisher anymore to publish a book, and you can upload your own films on YouTube whenever you like. In many cases, the internet has thus made the expert obsolete. Paradoxically, though, the internet has made it easier to assume the role of an expert. This automatically means that experts have become a less homogeneous group and the 'taste' of this group more diverse. If you want to go see a movie, you might not listen to the chief editor of the 'Culture' section of an established newspaper anymore, but prefer the opinion of a blogger who writes film reviews instead. Regardless of the democratised role of the expert, there will always be a specific group of experts that is taken more seriously in their assessment of new ideas than others.

Conservative by nature

In addition to generally having comparable judgments, experts are conservative by nature. When the experts of a domain are confronted with radical change, they are usually inclined to reject it. This is what happened to every new genre trying to enter the music domain, such as *jazz* and *rock and roll*. It is only human to reject change, though, as our brain has an evolutionary and thus inherent fear of the unknown. This is due to the efficient nature of our brain; it likes to be able to constantly predict what is to happen next and prefers to use past experiences, rather than new or ambiguous information, to do so. Another reason is the fear of social rejection and embarrassment. This is also an evolutionary remnant, since the human species – just as primates and the earliest homonids – is depended on the social group for survival. That's why human beings often unconsciously incorporate the opinion of the social group into their own opinion. The same happens in a group of experts with more or less similar tastes; they rather belong to the social group than have a dissenting opinion. It is thus also typically a social mechanism that keeps the subculture homogeneous. Finally, the experts are on average older than the creative minds that want to change a domain, which means they have an older brain. And the older a brain becomes, the harder it becomes biologically to abandon well-trodden knowledge tracks and patterns, perceive things differently and accept change. So, all in all, the experts form a serious barrier. Nevertheless, once the experts allow an idea to enter the creative domain, it will slowly – or, in today's world, increasingly quickly – be adopted by the masses.

In science, there is a long list of radical breakthroughs that were initially laughed at, while today these views are part of our common knowledge. Galileo was even punished by a Roman Catholic tribunal for stating that the earth was not the centre of the universe. Related 'radical' views that were initially strongly rejected are: the theory that the continents once formed a single continent and that they are constantly moving; the theory that a meteor killed the Dinosaurs; and the theory that our universe is expanding. Once an idea is adopted, it's hard to imagine what the domain looked like before it was.

Duchamp

Another example that illustrates how difficult it can be to enter an entirely new idea into a domain is the work of the French artist Marcel Duchamp. He was a member of *Dadaism*, an artistic-political movement in the beginning of the 20th century that rejected the prevailing definitions of art. The movement turned down reason and logic, and praised the concepts of nonsense, irrationality and intuition. Since the Dadaists criticised cultural and intellectual conformity, it is a good example of creativity introducing new ideas to the domain and thus changing it. Especially Duchamp became world-famous for it. In 1915, while living in New York, he invented a new form of art called *Readymades*. The genre presented objects that already had another purpose as works of art. Duchamp's most famous readymade was a porcelain urinal turned on its back, titled *Fountain*, and signed with the pseudonym, "R. Mutt 1917".

Duchamp submitted his fountain to an exhibition hosted by the *Society of Independent Artists*, a collective of *avant-garde* artists, of which he was a member himself. Avant-garde, a term derived from the foremost part of an army advancing into battle, was an experimental and innovative movement, influenced by Dadaism. Duchamp wanted to stay anonymous with his submission to challenge the progressiveness of the Society and see how far they were willing to stretch the definition of art. Though the avant-garde artists prided themselves for their progressiveness, claiming that their exhibitions were open to anyone who wanted to display a work of art, Duchamp's Fountain was rejected. According to the Society Fountain was not new; it was a urinal that had already been created by someone else. Displaying it on its back didn't and couldn't transform it into a piece of art. Disappointed by their rigidity, Duchamp resigned from the Society. Shortly after this incident the 'urinal' was bought by a wealthy collector which changed its status almost overnight. The collector functioned as the expert who allowed the urinal to enter the creative domain.

Today, Fountain is considered a landmark of 20th-century art. Some even say it planted the first seed for modern art – in particular conceptual art – because it stretched the definition of art and inspired artists to venture into new artistic directions. Just like in the scientific domain, the artistic domain has a great number of examples of art that was initially rejected. The first *impressionist* paintings, just like Duchamp's work, were not allowed to enter official exhibitions. In fact, 'impressionism' was a derogative term, since experts judged the works as merely giving an impression. Today, impressionism is one of the most-admired art movements in the world.

The opposite also occurs; a new idea seems substantial at the time it enters a domain, while today it is considered quite insignificant. This proves that time easily changes our opinion – both positively and negatively. Paradoxically, however, 50 years from now, even the most diverse works from the same creative domain will begin to look quite homogeneous. This could suggest that in hindsight each work from the same era should be valued similarly. Since this is clearly not the case, and some creative minds have more success than their contemporaries who create very similar works shows that timing and luck, and – as we will see in the next chapters – personality and skill are very important factors in creating historical works.

Ahead of time

Even though you might expect the scientific domains to be less flexible, as novelty and value are measured along more objective scientific laws, the mechanism involved in experts deciding whether or not new ideas are to enter the domain is very similar. What's more, taste, beliefs, and personal favours are often just as important as in the artistic domains. Gregor Mendel, for example, an Augustinian friar, born in the Austrian Empire – now the Czech Republic – and known today as the 'father of modern genetics,' published an article in 1866 that explained the theory of discontinuous inheritance, meaning that even if both your parents have brown eyes, you can still have blue eyes if one of your grandparents or great-grandparents had blue eyes. The leading scholars in the field were not impressed by his study on pea plants which substantiated his theory and his paper which explained his findings. Even though he was scientifically disciplined, conducting his research conscientiously over a period of 8 years on no less than 30,000 pea plants and writing a thorough paper, his humble background and the fact that he grew his pea plants in the monastery's kitchen garden probably didn't help his credibility. Because Mendel's peers didn't take his work seriously, it was reduced to just another theory on heredity. It took 35 years before other botanists, who conducted similar studies, rediscovered Mendel's work.

What Mendel's example show is that sometimes the domain doesn't seem to be ready to accept a new idea. Some artists or scientists are too far ahead of their time and thus cannot get their work to be appreciated. Just like Van Gogh, Mendel never got to enjoy the success of being valued by the masses. Only 16 years after his death, the domain showed appreciation for his work. In Duchamp's case, the domain was in the process of moving into a new direction; the Dadaists had already introduced a new set of rules that accepted a looser definition of art. You could say that the time was ripe for someone to shake up the domain and radically redefine art.

Superorganism

What's particularly interesting about the timing of ideas is that when a domain is ready for a new idea, similar ideas might suddenly pop up in several different places at the same time. Even though Western society tends to focus on the individual as the sole genius behind a creative idea, and even though the experts play an important role in allowing an idea to change a domain, each creative domain is a cultural entity with many different powers that influence the adoption of ideas. Especially the introduction of the internet has made these powers more complex, less hierarchical and more fluent. So, regardless of the specific roles of the creator, the expert, and the audience, a creative domain is an organic structure that also values and adopts ideas as a kind of superorganism. This doesn't mean that the individual is irrelevant for changing the domain; it just means that the creative domain as a whole needs to be ready for an idea in order for it to be changed.

4.

Motivated by Personality

*The most seductive thing about art
is the personality of the artist himself*

Paul Cézanne

Well-connected

Even though a creative domain as a whole needs to be ready for certain ideas, the personality of the creator also plays an important role in the value that is given to new ideas. Van Gogh and Picasso were both regarded as the most famous and influential painters of early 20th century. However, during their lives only Picasso was successful. Picasso reached a wide audience and sold many of his works, while during his life Van Gogh was only able to sell his works to his brother Theo. One of the reasons for this is that Picasso started his career at a much earlier age than Van Gogh. When Van Gogh died, aged 37, he had only been painting for about 7 years. Picasso was 9 when he started painting and had already been receiving formal artistic training from his father for two years. At that time, Picasso still had more than 80 years of painting ahead of him. That's how, over the span of his entire life, he was able to make some 13,000 paintings and around 300 sculptures.

Apart from age, there was another important reason for the difference in success. Van Gogh was quite introverted, living for his work and not much occupied with networking. Businesswise, Van Gogh's only link to the 'outside' world was his brother. In contrast, the charismatic Picasso enjoyed socialising, knew how to charm people, and for that reason had many friends in multiple social circles. He mingled with artists, writers, and politicians. This made him a well-known and respected person which helped him to sell his work. This difference doesn't necessarily mean that Picasso was more talented than Van Gogh. It merely shows how being social, well-connected, and building a profile can help with getting the artist's work to be considered of value.

Intrinsic versus extrinsic

The difference between people who couldn't care less what the outside world values and people with social antennas, knowing exactly how to please an audience, is similar to the difference between intrinsic and extrinsic motivation. Intrinsic motivation drives people to create for the mere challenge, enjoyment or satisfaction, or more simply put: for themselves. Extrinsic motivation, aiming at receiving a positive evaluation or reward, takes into account what the outside world appreciates. Both can help the creative process, but most studies have shown that intrinsic motivation is far more important. Extrinsic motivation can even easily be detrimental to the creative process. Working for an external reward often comes with external influence. After all, those who pay for creativity often want their view incorporated in the creative product in one way or another. This frustrates the autonomous nature of the intrinsic motivation. So even Picasso, who was more aware than Van Gogh with whom he should become friends, was still primarily driven by his intrinsic motivation. If not, he would have never been able to develop so strongly throughout his career. In fact, this is one of the strongest indicators for Picasso's extraordinary creative talent. If the people surrounding him and buying his works had been too strong an influence, he would probably have been slowed down in his development and would have demonstrated less diversity in his work.

Both intrinsic and extrinsic motivation can be linked to certain personality traits. Social characteristics, such as extraversion (aiming to obtain gratification from what is outside the self) and empathy and reflective self-criticism (reviewing your own work from a different perspective) are important for understanding how a work fits in the domain and how it can be sold. In contrast, intrinsic motivation is often linked to personality traits such as optimism, self-confidence, autonomy, perfectionism, non-conformism, and persistence. Unlike social skills, these traits help the creative mind to avoid distraction or influence from the rules and experts that define the domain.

Because intrinsic motivation is so much more important for creativity, it's no coincidence that we often associate the creative mind with a solitary person, living in his or her own world and not caring about the people surrounding him or her. Which, by the way, was clearly the other, non-social side to Picasso's personality. This is also how one of the greatest filmmakers ever, the American Stanley Kubrick, was described. Kubrick was not just called a recluse, who rarely did an interview, but also an obsessive, compulsive, demanding, and megalomaniac control freak. Although these negative personality traits made him hard to work with, they were also essential to him becoming a great director. A director who reinvented several very different genres, such as *war* (*Paths of Glory* and *Full Metal Jacket*), *science fiction* (*2001: A Space Odyssey*), and *thriller* (*The Shining*). When making a new movie, he would completely immerse himself in the genre and involve himself in every meticulous detail of the film such as the script, the actors, the production design, the costumes, the cinematography, the music, and the editing. He often drove his actors mad by doing a scene in 50 takes; less than perfect was never good enough. However, as intrinsically driven as he was, bad reviews always affected him. He wanted his movies to be both artistic and commercial successes. Which shows that even the most autonomous creator is affected by extrinsic forces and understands their importance.

Flow

One of the strongest intrinsic motivators of all is called *flow*, a condition during which artists, inventors, and scientists are in a state of being completely focused on the creative process and not thinking about irrelevant matters. When the creative mind is in flow, it is completely consumed by the work at hand, fully concentrated, optimally challenged, and not worrying about things such as physical conditions, personal problems, external opinions, and time. So, during the state of flow one typically completely forgets to have lunch or suddenly realises it's already dark outside. The state of flow is caused by a release of dopamine in the brain which works as a neurotransmitter with a very powerful effect on attention, which is why it's so easy to focus during the state of flow. But the dopamine doesn't just help us to focus, it turns the state of flow into a very pleasurable experience; an experience very similar to the addictive rush felt by a trained athlete during physical exertion. Therefore, the one thing all creative minds have in common is that they love what they do when they're fully occupied doing it. It is the state of flow that supports the saying *"it's about the journey, not the destination."* This satisfactory feeling of the journey is what Alfred Hitchcock described when he was asked what his definition of happiness was: *"Nothing to worry about on your plate. Only things that are creative, not destructive. When you can look forward and the road is clear ahead. And now you're going to create something."* The link between happiness and creativity is also made in scientific research which has shown that people that score higher on a standard measure of happiness, score up to 25% better with regard to solving creative puzzles.

When you look at the state of flow from an evolutionary perspective, it has a higher purpose than just being pleasant. Similarly to eating and having sex, the pleasure of being in flow suits the purpose of survival. Even though wandering off the beaten track could easily get our far-away ancestors killed, with danger lurking behind every new corner, the reward of discovering new plants, animals, and tools gave the more adventurous individual or group an advantage over the others. So, despite our evolutionary fear of the unknown, we have a nervous system in which the discovery of novel things stimulates the pleasure centres in the brain. Therefore, when we *do* come across new things and methods, we get rewarded. While creative minds generally have a bigger drive to explore new things, during adolescence, most people have this drive. This is a mechanism also displayed in the animal kingdom which helps a species to adapt more quickly to new environments.

Open mind

In addition to the motivational personality traits and the state of flow that helps the creative mind to relentlessly pursue an idea, there's another important set of character traits that often comes in handy a bit earlier on in the creative process; curiosity and imagination. The first one feeds the brain with knowledge and the second one – as we already learned in chapter 1 – is able to transform it. Curiosity is concerned with being sensitive to stimuli, open-minded, eager to learn, and having an eye for detail. Imagination is concerned with having a flexible and associative mind. All of these traits are strongly represented in children, who constantly try to make sense of the world around them by touching everything, experimenting, and imagining things that are generally regarded as impossible. If you split the act of creation into curiosity and imagination on the one hand, and the translation of an idea into a medium on the other, then a creative mind requires the open-minded imagination of a child to see the impossible and the focus and dedication of an adult to transform the impossible into reality.

Mood disorders

It's due to the opposite extremes of being curious and imaginative on the one hand and focused and productive on the other that has given the more creative minds in this world a 10 times bigger chance of being bipolar. Bipolarity – or manic depression – is an affective disorder that makes people oscillate between extreme euphoria and intense sadness. It is during the optimistic state that bipolarity helps the creative mind to be visionary and see that the sky is the limit. During the melancholic state, however, the same person becomes unsocial, locks himself up and becomes completely occupied with the execution of an idea. Apart from bipolarity, highly creative individuals are generally more often diagnosed with mood disorders.

Another way to look at mood disorders in relation to creativity is that the self-actualisation and self-expression most people find in creativity provides a way to cope with strong and conflicting emotions. Which means that creativity can help to channel these emotions – similar to how self-disclosure, being a standard part of psychotherapy, helps one to organise one's emotions. When you look at it from this perspective, creativity can simply be seen as a byproduct of a mood disorder instead of the other way around.

In addition to being a visionary, *Apple* founder Steve Jobs, who just like Stanley Kubrick was something of a control freak, was also known for his difficult personality. His moods were quickly changeable and could switch from being extremely rude, arrogant, manipulative, and even childish – he would often start to cry if he didn't get his way – to being intensely friendly, charismatic, and courteous – mainly when he needed to cajole someone into something. Although incredibly unsympathetic, Jobs could have never made Apple into the most valuable company in the world without his personality. He used both ends of the spectrum – his huge ego as well as his charm – to get things done and turn his imagination into reality.

27 Club

Mood disorders don't just stimulate creativity. Naturally, they can also be quite destructive. Especially artists are known for being more sensitive and emotional in their behaviour. One of the reasons is that, compared to scientists who are focused on the external world, artists are often on a more introspective journey. Van Gogh cutting off his ear is a famous example, but many rock and pop stars are known to lead risky lives, experiment with drugs, and commit suicide more commonly. Good examples of this are the musicians Brian Jones, Jimi Hendrix, Janis Joplin, Jim Morrison, Kurt Cobain, and Amy Winehouse, who all famously died at the young age of 27, directly or indirectly as a result of drug and alcohol abuse. It's hard to say whether the '27 Club' were prone to experimenting with drugs because of their personality, or whether their personality changed because of their drug habit, but there is a correlation between the creative personality and the attraction towards drugs.

Although drugs usually don't help the creative mind when used in large quantities and addictively, from the perspective of creativity it can have positive effects in the short term. It can help the creator to be more confident – thus reducing the fear of failure – or sociable. Moreover, it can enhance the ability to imagine or be productive. More specifically, cannabis, for example, stimulates the making of associations, which makes categorising knowledge in new ways easier – the disadvantage being that paying attention becomes more difficult. Alcohol can also induce sociable behaviour, so that people more easily connect to others. Amphetamines increase the release of dopamine in the brain, which helps the creative mind to be completely focused on the work at hand. The artificial state of flow this drug causes is not just pleasurable, it's also very useful for working long periods of time on one single project. A famous example is Jack Kerouac, who wrote *On the Road* during a three-week writing session with eighteen-hour days, thanks to the amphetamine *Benzedrine*.

Jackson Pollock

Though there are many different personality traits and mood states that can help the creator in the creative process, the audience of a creative domain can also be of influence. This external influence can stimulate the creator, but as is the case with drugs, too much of it is likely to influence the creator negatively. The downside of an audience, especially in the artistic domain, is that they'd rather consume the work of an eccentric than that of a dull personality. Most journalists, who function as experts, also would rather write about someone that deviates from the norm. They thus create a culture in which the artist scores better when behaving abnormal.

Eccentricity in art started in the late Renaissance, when artists became celebrities for the first time. In 1550, the art history writer Giorgio Vasari complained how the new generation of artists had changed into a mad and savage species, whereas in the early Renaissance artists were still tame and sensible. Later on, in the 18th Century, *Romanticism* further nurtured the expectations around artists' eccentric behaviour. The Romantics strongly believed that rational deliberation killed the creative impulse and that creativity was not founded on the mastery of academic skills, but on one's imagination. So instead of being a craftsman controlled by conscious deliberation, the artist simply had to listen to their inner self and create with emotion and on instinct. The starving poet or alcoholic writer became more credible than those who saw creativity as a craft.

When looking at the life and work of American painter Jackson Pollock, the parallels between him and the Romantic definition of the emotional, sensitive, and instinctive artist are striking. Pollock's life was saturated with depression, self-doubt, and alcohol, that latter of which resulted in a fatal car accident at the age of 44. He was also known for his troubled marriage, his infidelity, and – most saliently – for urinating in Peggy Guggenheim's fireplace. Pollock became known for his technique of painting, later dubbed 'action painting.' Seemingly bordering on madness, he danced around a huge canvas that was lying on the floor and threw his paint across it. Pollock claimed that while painting he was actually *in* his painting, not aware of what he was doing and being in pure harmony with his work. Though this sounds like the perfect state of flow, and though he did introduce a *new* technique of painting – making him undeniably creative – his extraordinary performance also helped him to sell his work. Thus it was not just his mood disorder that made him create like a madman; it was also the attention his eccentricity generated among his audience that stimulated his behaviour.

Just as in Kubrick's case, the example of Pollock shows there is always an interplay between the intrinsic drive of the creator and the extrinsic world around him, appreciating eccentricity. However, those creative minds that are primarily driven by extrinsic gratification aren't truly creative. The intrinsic drive to create should always be the strongest motivator.

5.

Mastering the Rules

It's not wise to violate rules,
until you know how to observe them

Thomas Stearns Eliot

Renaissance Man

The personality traits that help us in the creative process are for the most part innate, residing our in brain from birth. But the basis of all creativity, knowledge, is not innate; it is gathered slowly, through using our senses, experimenting, learning, and interacting with others. Knowledge is essential for being creative. After all, if you want to change a creative domain you need to learn how it is defined. The better you understand the domain, the easier it becomes to play with the rules within that domain.

If there is one person in the history of creative geniuses that is known for his extensive knowledge, it is Leonardo da Vinci. He was a walking encyclopaedia. Quite literally; he wrote down and drew all the observations and theories he gathered from the world around him in endless notes, most of them written in mirror. What's interesting about Da Vinci is that he was knowledgeable in a wide variety of domains. That's why he is often called a *Renaissance Man*. Renaissance is derived from the French *renaître*, meaning to be born again. From the 14th century onwards, mankind was said to be reborn, as from then on there was an awareness of the fact that human beings have the unique talent of absorbing knowledge and thus the capacity to develop autonomously, rather than being solely formed by external forces. Compared to the destructive Middles Ages, in our collective memory dominated by famine, plagues, and war, the Renaissance was a time of cultural and creative prosperity.

Technical and cultural rules

There are two kinds of knowledge we can gather in order to be creative within a certain domain; technical knowledge and cultural knowledge. Technical knowledge allows us to operate and create within a specific domain. Cultural knowledge allows us to understand the symbols and conventions of the domain and to anticipate on how experts and audiences will value new ideas presented to the domain. When you become a photographer, you first need to learn some technical rules: how to operate a camera, how light influences the sensor, and how to manipulate photos. Then, in terms of culture, you first learn about the famous photographers of the domain and why they are valued. After you've learned these basic rules – often through formal schooling – you become further enriched with knowledge on the job, by practice and interaction with peers and audiences. Once you start to understand the nuances of the domain and discover your specific qualities, you adopt a personal style and form a vision of your position in the creative domain.

The technical and cultural rules are closely related; a change in technique can influence the culture, and vice versa. Take the digitalisation of photography, for instance. It democratised the domain by making cameras and imaging software more easily accessible. Along with that came the ease of distribution of photos through the internet, which strongly increased the number of photos being spread. This changed the cultural dynamics of the domain. The analogue grain, for example, has become scarcer than the pixel, which is why in galleries analogue prints are often valued higher than digital print and which has led to the situation that digital photos are occasionally turned into analogue film before being printed. Though technically the grain conveys a different sharpness, there is definitely a touch of cultural nostalgia in preferring the grain. It's the imperfection of analogue that turned *Polaroid* and *Lomo* into fashionable retro brands, similar to how the crackle in vinyl became attractive after the introduction of the CD. This shows how the changes in technical and cultural rules go hand in hand.

Sampling

Digitalisation has not just innovated the domain of photography. It has produced new tools in many different domains and changed the technical rules within these domains. Since creative minds are generally more open to change than others, new rules stimulate experimentation and creative production and therefore shake up a domain as if it were is under construction again. An example of a domain that has changed much more radically through digitalisation is the musical domain. An essential first step in this change was the invention of *sampling*; a technique invented at the end of the 70s, making it possible to digitalise segments of music, loop them, and incorporate them into another recording. Sampling made *hip hop* possible, and hip hop became such a popular new music genre that it even turned into an entire subculture with break dancing, graffiti art, and a sneaker revolution – again proving that technical innovations also have a cultural impact. Sampling was an essential building block for many new musical subdomains, thus changing the entire musical landscape.

Another new subdomain was largely made possible by the Japanese music hardware manufacturer *Roland*. At the start of the 80s it presented the *TB-303*, a bassline synthesiser introduced to replace the bass guitar. This instrument, together with Roland's drum machine, unintentionally laid down the foundation for electronic dance music. What Roland hadn't foreseen when creating the '303' was that it had strong improvisational limitations. It couldn't be played as freely as a bass guitar, making it an unattractive replacement. But those who experimented with it soon enough found out that the 303 allowed them to distort the bass sound and change parameters such as pitch and filtering into registers beyond the traditional bass. It then became famous for that which it was perfectly able to do: rapidly repeating note patterns over and over again. Together with the possibilities of the drum machine, samplers, and mixers a series of completely new music genres was created, such as *acid house*, *techno*, *jungle*, and *drum and bass*. A great example of how the experimental drive of creative minds makes it hard to predict in what direction new tools and technical rules will take a domain.

Skill

Being knowledgeable and having the right tools both help us at least to properly apply the rules that define a domain. However, actually creating something that stands out requires skill. It is skill that allows one to create with ease and distinctive capacity. It is also what lifted Da Vinci above being 'merely' an exceptionally smart theorist. It was the combination of knowledge *and* skill that turned him into an outstanding scientist, painter, sculptor, musician, architect, engineer, builder, cartographer, botanist and writer.

To become skilful in a certain creative domain it first of all helps to be talented. Unlike knowledge, which is slowly acquired through learning, talent is innate and usually reveals itself at a young age. Wolfgang Amadeus Mozart, for example, was a musical talent, who could already play the piano at age four and started composing when he was six. Musical talent is one of the eight cognitive abilities that are useful for being creative in a domain. The other abilities are linguistic, spatial, mathematical, naturalist, bodily kinesthetic, interpersonal, and intrapersonal talent. The separation between these creative talents is not that strict; some overlap and most of them can be used in several domains. But there are differences. An architect is talented at working with spaces, while the poet can juggle with language.

Unlike Da Vinci, most creative minds reveal talent in one or maybe, if they're lucky, a few creative domains. Those who are talented in more than one domain are usually talented at related ones. So while a scientist can easily make a good musician or chess player, a linguistic talent will statistically more often show interpersonal qualities as well. What's interesting about the different creative talents is that they are not bound by culture, since our cognitive abilities are shaped by evolution, which means they have been – and still are – useful in our survival and reproductive success. With language, for example, you can write poems or letters that impress and seduce a member of the other sex.

Even more important than talent in acquiring skill is practice. It is easily possible to compensate a lack of talent with endless practice, while inversely it's impossible for a talented person to become a master at something without much practice. Even talents such as Mozart could only become world-famous through huge amounts of practice. Research shows that you need roughly 10,000 hours of practice to achieve the level of skill of a 'world-class player.' That goes for all creative domains in which skill plays an important role, e.g. the domain of graphic design, ballet, chess, music, basketball, or programming – to name but a few.

Creative peak

Our talent for applying certain skills doesn't fluctuate much during our lives. But the exact time at which we peak creatively depends on our personal learning curve. Van Gogh only started painting when he was 30, but once he got a taste for it, he became extremely productive and went through a very steep learning curve. Within a period of only seven years he changed from an amateur painter who didn't seem extremely talented into a skilled painter with his very own technique. Different painters have different peaks. If you take the value given to a work to-day as an indicator for one's creativity, then Picasso peaked in his mid-twenties, while French *post-impressionist* Paul Cézanne peaked in his mid-sixties.

Regardless of the individual differences, what most creative minds have in common is that their creative productivity and success displays an inverted-U function of the acquired knowledge of the domain. Which means that as you learn more about the rules of the domain, your creative potential grows. At some point, however, when your peak has been reached, the naive perspective and drive that makes the youth want to change the world is increasingly replaced by a mind that has narrowed down, gets stuck in patterns, and is not able deviate from the rules anymore. Which is why the established experts in a domain quickly take a conservative standpoint towards radical changes in a domain.

Each creative domain has its own characteristic inverted-U, depending on how strictly defined the knowledge of a domain is. Domains with a clear and logically consistent body of knowledge have an earlier peak age than the more loosely defined domains with more ambiguous rules. Therefore poets and chess players tend to peak in their 20s, while geologists and biologists do so much later, often not until their 40s or even 50s. The average peak may change when the rules of a domain change. For example, when the domain becomes more complicated, more popular, or valued differently. Which is why the difference between Picasso's and Cézanne's peak is actually somewhat misleading. Cézanne was born 40 years before Picasso and when you compare them to other painters in France, you will find that those born early in the 19th century peaked later in life, while painters born closer to the 20th century peaked earlier in life.

Mozart

The combination of having to learn the rules of the domain and practice for some 10,000 hours ensures that children, however talented, cannot become *historically* creative at a very young age. This doesn't mean they can't be *personally* creative. In fact, as we've learned in the previous chapter, when it comes to curiosity and imagination, children can easily be more creative than adults. The reason being that their brain is still flexible and unhindered by formal education or conventions, allowing them to create their own rules and fantasy worlds. But because they don't fully master the technical and cultural rules of the domain yet, they are not able to produce culturally relevant works. Therefore, you hardly see their works in a museum or performed in a concert hall, unless especially meant for family and friends. So, even prodigies like Mozart who technically master a piano at a very young age still need to learn and understand the culture of the domain. That's why Mozart's earliest pieces were merely arrangements of works by other composers. It was not until he was 21 that he wrote what today is considered a masterpiece: No. 9, K. 271. At that age, he started to understand how his peers and predecessors followed and broke the rules in the domain and was able to claim his own position in the domain.

So, becoming historically creative within a creative domain requires a lot from the creative mind. First of all, you need to adopt the technical and cultural rules of the domain. Furthermore, you need some talent to become skilful within a domain. But whatever the degree of talent, you always need an incredible amount of practice. The paradox, though, is that the better you master the rules of the domain, the more difficult it becomes to think beyond them.

6.

Unfamiliar Combinations

It's not where you take things from
- it's where you take them

Jean - Luc Godard

The Periodic Table

Leonardo da Vinci was not just such a strong, creative mind because of his extensive knowledge of many different creative domains, topped off with a strong set of cognitive talents. It was also his ability to use his knowledge across various domains. His elaborate scientific studies, for example, not only helped him to invent new tools and theories, but also helped him in his art. From the world-famous *Mona Lisa*, painted between 1503 and 1516, it is quite apparent that Da Vinci knew more than other artists did about human anatomy, the course of light hitting a curved surface, and the illusion of depth on a two-dimensional surface. While mastering the knowledge of a specific domain is essential for being creative within this domain, the key to creativity is combining your knowledge with seemingly domain-irrelevant knowledge. In other words: creativity is about making an unfamiliar combination of familiar ideas.

Dmitri Mendeleyev's *Periodic Table*, presented for the first time in 1869, is a good example of an invention that incorporated domain-irrelevant knowledge. This tabular arrangement of the chemical elements is organised on the basis of the elements' atomic numbers, electron configurations, and recurring chemical properties. Mendeleyev's table arranges the chemical elements in such a simple and orderly way that it is still used today. Arranging the elements by weight had already been done a few years earlier. Arranging them by valence (the degree of combining power), too. What made Mendeleyev's diagram unique is that he combined these two arrangements into one scheme. When the diagram is read horizontally, from left to right, the elements are ordered by increasing weight and when read vertically by similar chemical properties. So vertically, for example, there is a group containing copper, gold, and silver, i.e. metals, and another group containing neon, helium, and argon, i.e. gases. The model works so well that any element discovered after its invention fit in perfectly and any element that is still to be discovered is likely to fit in, too. Mendeleyev's inspiration for his table came from the card game solitaire (or patience), in which cards are arranged by suit horizontally and by number vertically. Mendeleyev thus combined two existing ideas, the chemical elements and a trivial card game, into an unfamiliar combination.

Einstein

To be able to make unfamiliar combinations, one needs a flexible and associative mind that can fluently switch between and combine different sets of knowledge. More than our language and ability to make tools, this is what makes us unique as a species. Another genius famous for making unfamiliar combinations of familiar ideas was the physicist Albert Einstein. He couldn't have conceived of his groundbreaking *General Theory of Relativity*, if he hadn't been able to fluently move between the domains he was knowledgeable in. His theory on gravitation combines the knowledge of the logical-mathematical domain – allowing Einstein to recognise numerical patterns – and the spatial domain – allowing him to understand the physical world around him and its transformations. Einstein wasn't particularly talented in these domains; his academic record was good, but not excellent compared to some of the other students in his class. It was his ability to see connections between different domains and use his imagination to combine and transform them that made him a genius.

When we compare Da Vinci with Einstein it is interesting to note that in hindsight Einstein's knowledge went deeper and was thus more advanced than Da Vinci's. The reason for this is that in Einstein's time the total amount of knowledge available had grown exponentially compared to the Renaissance. The same applies to when we compare today's knowledge of physics to that of Einstein's. The knowledge we gather, formalise, and share as human beings never diminishes, but only increases. To illustrate this; in 1670, there was one single journal of science, and all of science was generally categorised under the heading 'natural history.' Today, the number of scientific titles is endless and keeps on growing. Which is why you can spend your entire life within the creative domain of physics and still not master all the different subdomains. With so many highly specialised subdomains nowadays, it is impossible to be as knowledgeable as Da Vinci was across so many different creative domains. Since the creative subdomains constantly evolve, are divided, and become more specialised, it is better to speak of 'conceptual domains' in the context of making unfamiliar combinations. A conceptual domain is basically a knowledge structure and can, even easier than the creative domain, be as small as you define it – e.g. how to prune an apple tree?

Graceland

Apart from the specialised knowledge belonging to a specific conceptual domain, we also need a large 'database' of general knowledge. After all, that is the knowledge that has the potential to become one of the halves of the unfamiliar combination. The broader your knowledge database, the bigger the chance you'll come across something that is useful in the conceptual domain you're working in. That's why, apart from a flexible and imaginative mind, you also need to be curious, eager to learn and knowledgeable about the world around you. Curiosity is what distinguishes Da Vinci and Einstein (*"I have no talent. I am only passionately curious"*) from the hyper-intelligent mind that

    Chapter 6

dedicates its life to one single, highly specialised conceptual domain without ever wandering outside it. Both curiosity and the eagerness to learn is what prevents them from becoming complacent, pushes them outside their comfort zone, and allows them to constantly evolve.

Musical artists such as David Bowie and Madonna clearly demonstrate this constant development throughout their careers. However, a more specific example of what can come from leaving your comfort zone is Paul Simon's most successful album *Graceland*, released in 1986. After the 1983 album *Hearts and Bones* proved a commercial failure, Simon decided to radically change his course. Essentially, he was a poppy folk singer, but a tape by the African band the *Boyoyo Boys* he once stumbled upon made him travel to South Africa to work with local bands and thus learn more about the musical roots of South Africa. This is how Graceland came to combine Western musical genres, such as rock, pop, and folk, with South African Zulu genres such as *isicathamiya* and *mbaqanga*. It would have been a lot easier to stay in New York and create the album in his familiar surroundings. Especially since Simon had to break the UN cultural boycott that was to fight racial segregation and decreed that no artist would work in South Africa. But it was the complete immersion in another culture that eventually created the perfect synthesis of two cultures. Ironically, the power of this cultural combination even influenced the UN in cancelling the cultural boycott.

What's in a name?

When we zoom in on unfamiliar combinations, the key to making one is seeing the bridge between different conceptual domains. This bridge is built through an analogy; idea A is like idea B. A famous experiment with a chimpanzee, conducted by

Wolfgang Köhler in 1918, illustrates in a very rudimentary way how analogies can lead to creative behaviour. Köhler put a (female) chimp in a cage with a stick that she could play with. Then some fruits were presented to the chimp outside the cage. When the chimp found out she couldn't reach the fruits she started whimpering and throwing herself on the ground out of frustration. A few moments later, she glanced at the stick, stopped moaning, seized the stick and succeeded, somewhat clumsily, to draw the fruit nearer to her, within arm's length. She was now able to reach the fruit directly through the bars of the cage. So whereas the chimp initially merely played with the stick, she then discovered it could also be used as a tool. The analogy being: the stick is like a tool. Similarly, Homo erectus described in chapter 1 at one point realised; the stone is like an axe. What analogies thus basically do is use the imagination to perceive things differently.

Combining the knowledge from two different conceptual domains through an analogy is also what Gutenberg did when he imagined he could use the screw of a wine press as the essential part of the printing press. And when architect Jørn Utzon imagined the *Sydney Opera House* he combined the conceptual domain of sailing with that of architecture, turning his building into one of the most unique architectural structures in the world. With regard to words, analogies are even easier to make. Which is why poets and writers make them constantly. Take Shakespeare's famous line from Romeo and Juliette: *"What's in a name? That which we call a rose. By any other name would smell as sweet."* Shakespeare made an analogy between Romeo Montague and a rose. Though Julia was to hate anyone with the name Montague, she reasoned that it didn't matter what Romeo's surname was because a rose smells great, regardless of what you call it. Romeo was like a rose. It shows how a simple analogy can become world-famous.

Since creativity is everywhere, analogies are too. The way animals are built, for example, is something that constantly inspires scientists and industrial designers for devising new scientific laws, tools, objects, and mechanisms that work more efficiently than their predecessors. An example is the unique quality of a shark's skin; it's abrasive, like sandpaper, due to a special type of scale, with small ridges, arranged like shingles. These ridges decrease drag in water and prevent particles from attaching to the shark. This unique feature explains the enormous speed that most sharks can reach with minimal effort. The structure of the shark's skin has been copied in special coatings for boats and in the fabric of swimsuits to improve the aerodynamics and reduce drag. The coating or the suit is like the skin of the shark.

Game of chess

As we've seen in the previous chapter, in some creative domains it's easier to make unfamiliar combinations than in others. This largely depends on the simplicity and rigidity of the rules that define it. Take the game of chess, for instance; it only has a few, logical rules that can be explained in a few minutes. Though it requires a lot of spatial talent and an extremely good visual memory to play chess, there's less room on a chessboard for creativity than, let's say, a blank canvas. While the chess player is restricted by horizontal and diagonal lines, the painter has an unlimited number of 'moves' on his canvas. The decisions in chess are therefore of a more binary nature. Which is why a computer program can hold the world title in chess, but no computer program has its own art exhibitions yet. This is not to say that the chess player can't be creative. He certainly can be by combining different chess patterns, and thus making a series of unexpected moves. But the margins for being creative are limited, because the number of moves is limited. The same goes for mathematicians. If $a^2 + b^2 = c^2$, there's only a limited number of possibilities to solve the equation. Again, this doesn't mean that a mathematician cannot be creative in the way he approaches a numerical problem. In fact, there are well over 300 different theories that prove the *Pythagorean* equation. It does mean, however, that creativity in the mathematical playing field is limited compared to domains with more flexible rules.

More generally, the difference between most scientific domains and most artistic domains, is the objectivity of the rules that define the domain. While the scientist tries to find and express an objective view – or truth – that explains the world, the artist expresses his own subjective view on the world. So, in the artistic domain the conceptual artist Michael Craig-Martin was able to become famous for displaying a glass of water and telling his audience that, as much as anything else, it is an oak tree – in order to explain that art only exists in the mind of the viewer. In the scientific domain some substantial, objective proof would have been required to make this work valuable.

Surprising

Regardless of the type of creative domain, an important element that influences the potential success of a combination is the obviousness of the combination. You might expect that the more subdomains there are, the easier it is to make creative combinations. The omnipresence and digitalisation of music, and accessibility of mix software, for example, has generated a myriad of genres. Combining them has therefore become much easier, subtler, and more fluent. As we've seen in chapter 2, though, the accessibility of tools doesn't make people more creative; the majority of combinations still sound familiar and thus not necessarily creative. The closer different subdomains are related to each other, the bigger the chance that someone has made the combination before. This also means that a combination that evokes surprise has a bigger chance of being truly creative.

So, combining one's knowledge of the human anatomy with art during the Renaissance eventually became the signature of an entire era and therefore too obvious to be called creative. Combining American music with exotic Zulu music – from a country that was internationally isolated – evoked a lot of surprise, and could therefore easily stand out. But there is a fine balance between surprising and too surprising. A combination that surprises people too much can easily evoke disbelief and laughter or even anger and resistance, in which case it is either too far ahead of its time or simply a bad combination.

7.

Problem Solved

We can't solve problems
by using the same kind of thinking
we used when we created them

Albert Einstein

White matter

It is not difficult to see how Da Vinci, Mozart, and Van Gogh differed so much from each other in terms of cognitive abilities. A more interesting question is what they had in common. Did they all have a special 'creativity gene'? Researchers have been trying to find objective brain features that indicate creative potential. They even researched one of the most famous creative minds that ever lived. Soon after Einstein died, on April 18th 1955, researchers at *Princeton University* extensively studied his brain. But none of their studies clarified any significant biological differences from the average brain. In fact, Einstein's brain weighed only 1,230 grams, while the adult male average is about 1,400 grams – a significant difference.

The weight of our brain depends largely on our white matter, which serves as an intricate wire system connecting different regions of our brain and transporting information. When comparing it with a computer, the outer parts of the brain, the grey matter, represents the applications, while the white matter represents the network cables connecting them so they can work together. A high amount of white matter – among many other factors – supports our intelligence because it helps our brain to work efficiently. However, creativity is not so much about efficiency, but rather about inefficiency. You could say that less efficient networks have a bigger chance of connecting information that doesn't belong together, and induce unfamiliar combinations.

The amount of white matter in our brain is just one of many indicators of creativity. When we zoom out of the brain and look at behaviour, creative potential is not easily measured. One of the reasons for this is that creativity requires different mental processes, talents, skills, and personality traits at the same time. Being above averagely creative means you are intelligent, focused, imaginative, associative, self-confident, tenacious, etc. And while we all possess some of these qualities, having them all is what makes someone stand out creatively.

Testing creativity

Measuring one's creative potential by scanning the brain is still a bridge too far, but there are psychological tests that measure creative potential to a certain extent. The earliest tests aiming to establish creative potential were intelligence tests. The reason for this is that, originally, creativity was regarded as a by-product of high intelligence. This is not true, but there is an overlap between the two; creative minds get above-average scores on tests of general intelligence, with the exception of IQs of over about 120. Some features measured in IQ tests are important for being creative: learning abilities, the quality of one's short-term memory, analytical abilities, decision speed, etc. But creativity requires a very important ability that cannot be measured with a standard IQ test, and that is imagination. The difference between intelligence and imagination is that intelligence is predominantly used for convergent thinking, which means coming up with a single right answer through a process of analytical deduction, while imagination uses divergent thinking, which means coming up with as many potential answers as possible.

The first dedicated creativity tests were developed in the United States during World War II. The reason for focusing more specifically on creativity, rather than on general intelligence, was that the *US Airforce* regarded creative pilots as better suited to saving their own lives and planes when in unexpected situations. To test creative potential, the respondents were asked, for example, to name as many blue items or as many uses for a brick as possible, hereby testing whether they could think beyond the obvious pair of blue jeans, and throwing the brick through a window respectively. The new creativity tests thus essentially rewarded divergent thinking. Intelligence helps you to quickly sum up and tick off all the theoretical and procedural steps when flying a plane under relatively normal circumstances. Divergent thinking, however, is more useful at times when the tail of your plane is on fire as you are chased and attacked by hostile gunfire, and the joystick doesn't react adequately. Divergent thinking thus helps you to find a solution to a problem that was never covered during your formal training.

Houston, we've had a problem

So, when a problem occurs that lies outside the parameters of the textbook, creativity has a bigger chance of coming up with an adequate solution. That's, for example, how *Apollo 13* – not actually an aircraft, but a spacecraft – was saved after an oxygen tank exploded (*"Houston, we've had a problem"*) two days after its launch and prior to its planned lunar landing. The explosion damaged the Command Module, the cabin that housed the crew of three and was essential for re-entering the earth's atmosphere and safe landing in the Ocean. For the Space Centre in Houston, and even more for the crew on the Apollo 13, it was crucial to solve a series of problems they had never faced before, such as the way to abort the mission, the limited power supply, and the need for a makeshift repair of the damaged carbon dioxide removal system, making sure the crew wouldn't suffocate. It was creatively solving these problems that helped the Apollo 13 to safely return home.

Basically, any problem on any level of intelligence without any obvious solution requires creative thinking. Or, simply put, human beings tap into their creativity when they encounter a problem. Even the chimp in the previous chapter, turning a stick into a tool to reach the fruit outside her cage, needed creativity to find a solution. The obvious difference from the problems on Apollo 13 is that the mission's solutions came much closer to rocket science and were conceived more consciously than the chimp's relatively simple solution. What both problems have in common, though, is that they require productive, rather than reproductive thinking. Reproductive thinking only uses the available knowledge from past experiences that fit into the conceptual domain in a linear, analytical manner. Productive thinking creates new knowledge structures.

Finding problems

In the process of solving a problem, finding it is at least as important. Finding a problem comes down to identifying the right problem to solve and framing it in the right context. When you put problems in a different context, by questioning whether you are solving the right problem, the number and nature of possible solutions change along with the context. For example, if you want to cross a river, you can build a bridge. If this becomes problematic, you could ask yourself: "Why do I need to build a bridge? Why not swim across the river or use a canoe?" In this manner, you create a larger context for solving your problem and, by doing so, the problem changes. You can also ask yourself: "Do I really need to cross the river at this exact point?" When you walk along the river to find a better spot for crossing over, you might encounter a natural bridge which instantly solves the problem. You can even ask yourself: "Do I need to cross the river at all?" Questioning the problems you are trying to solve and thus finding new problems is the most important part of problem solving. It is why Einstein said that the really important breakthroughs in science are made through reformulating old problems or discovering new ones, rather than solving existing problems.

Fixed assumptions

Although theoretically this all makes much sense, in reality finding the right problem is not always easy. The reason for this is that our brain is ruled by fixed assumptions that are based on existing knowledge structures and past experiences. There are many seemingly simple puzzles that prove this point quite convincingly. Here's an example: Add one line to IX to make six. The reason why this puzzle could prove difficult is that you might assume that the problem needs to be solved in the context of Roman numerals, in which case you are looking at the figure for 9 which is impossible to convert into VI by adding one line. But when we step outside the context of Roman numerals and into that of the Roman alphabet, the problem becomes easy to solve. We simply put an 'S' in front of IX.

Our brain is inclined to pick the most likely interpretation for what it is seeing, because this is simply the most efficient way for our brain to work. From an evolutionary perspective, it saves computing power and energy when our perception makes statistical guesses about what we see, based on past experiences. And it doesn't just save energy, it also helps us distinguish between prey and predator and decide whether to fight or flee within tenths of seconds. The downside of these automatic thinking processes is that they prevent us from placing things into a different context. If most of our perceptions were nuanced and weighed in different contexts, we'd spend a lot more neural energy on scanning our surroundings. And though we have an incredibly efficient brain, it already uses 20% of our entire body's energy at times when we're more or less at rest.

 Chapter 7

Zooming in

In the process of reframing a problem, it is easy to generate more problems than you started out with in the first place. Generally, the further you zoom in on a problem, the more new problems you encounter. For example, the problem might start with a simple "What kind of building suits the harbour of Sydney?" Then, when the architect decides that it should resemble a sailing ship, he needs to ask himself: "What should the exact shape of the sails be?" When he zooms in on this problem, he'll come across a number of problems that have to do with topics such as geometry, materials, and construction. In fact, this proved the biggest problem in building the Sydney Opera House; creating the right construction to support the impressive roof. It took the design team from 1957 to 1963 and at least 12 versions of different shapes – among them parabolas, circular ribs, and three-dimensional ellipses – to find an economically acceptable form. But that was just the design. It was not until 1973 that the building was finally finished. The project proved so difficult that Jørn Utzon had to painfully resign in 1966, because he lost support among some of his co-creators and basically stopped receiving payment. Utzon's design clearly won due to its elegant simplicity, not due to the number of problems the execution caused.

Zooming in on a problem is what we particularly need to do when we face an ill-defined problem. "Sydney needs an opera house" is clearly ill-defined, since there are too many solutions. The more specific a problem is defined, the more direction we are given in finding a solution. Generally, the scientific domain works with problems that are better defined than the artistic domain. The autonomous poet, who starts with a blank piece of paper, can formulate his problem as vaguely as: 'I am in love and want to express my feelings.' But, as we've seen in Utzon's case, the freedom of being allowed to come up with many different solutions does not necessarily make the problem easier to solve. In fact, ill-defined problems require more divergent thinking and therefore a more productive brain.

Switching brain halves

Whatever the nature of a problem, both divergent and convergent thinking are used in the process of problem solving. The reason for this is that the creative process is always about divergently searching the conceptual domain for different solutions and convergently applying the technical and cultural rules of the domain to find the best solution. The sketch from Utzon came from divergent thinking, but the execution of the work convergently needed to apply the laws of gravitation and motion, to name just two. Even if you want to change a domain and think beyond the conventions, there always are rules that need to be applied; the words in a poem need to create harmony and a certain rhythm to be appreciated.

For divergent and convergent thinking we use very different parts of the brain. The right half of our brain is better at divergent thinking. More specifically, it is better at associative, holistic, spatial, and perceptual processes. Simply put; it is better at seeing the bigger picture. Because the right half of the brain has a broader and more sensitive perspective, it is used for imagination, producing dreams and dealing with emotions. Since the left brain is more analytical and has more eye for detail, it is more useful for convergent thinking. Or, in other words, for logical, deductive, and linear thinking. But even though each half of the brain has its own qualities, the creative process requires them to work together seamlessly through a bundle of roughly 100 million neurons. Neurons are nerve cells that are able to send messages to other neurons. This communicative collaboration is essential. Even the simple task of drawing a picture shows how both halves need each other; the left hemisphere captures the details, while the right hemisphere captures the overall image. The same goes for understanding a joke, irony, or a metaphor; while the left hemisphere analyses the literal text, the right hemisphere bridges the different elements, revealing the humour, smartness or beauty of the analogy. The right hemisphere is thus like the painter who takes a few steps back from his easel to zoom out and look at his entire work after he has been preoccupied with some of the 'left hemisphere' details.

Even though the scientist's analytical left brain might be better developed than the artist's right half, scientists also need the imagination of their right brain to be able to think outside the established rules of their conceptual domain. At the same time, while the artist's emotional and holistic right brain might be better developed than that of the scientist, the artist also needs to solve technical problems, such as: "What is the most efficient form for making a sail-shaped building?" The strongest creative minds don't just shine with one half of their brain; they use both halves to an equal extent. In fact, that's why it's so difficult to measure the creative potential of the human brain; we use our entire brain to solve creative problems.

8.

Preparing for Insights

Chance favours the prepared mind

Louis Pasteur

Suddenly illuminated

What is typical about a creative problem is that solving it always seems impossible; it's like a puzzle with an essential piece missing. This is what Watson and Crick experienced when they tried to construct the exact structure of our DNA. The many scientists who were competing to be the first to find the right solution, all more or less possessed the same pieces of the puzzle; they knew that our DNA is built up of two long-chain polymers (read: strings). They also knew that there are two different base pairs in the structure and how these pairs were and were not capable of chemically connecting with the strings. The only piece that was missing, was the exact structure: the double helix, which makes the strings intertwine like a spiral staircase, supported by the base pairs connecting perpendicularly to the strings.

Karl Popper once metaphorically described the search for the missing piece as a blind man searching a dark room for a black hat that might perhaps not even be there. This metaphor is striking, since the universal symbol for the moment at which we solve a problem is the light bulb. When the light bulb is turned on, the room becomes illuminated and we suddenly clearly see the solution. This moment is called the moment of *insight*.

Archimedes

From a cerebral standpoint, the moment of insight is the moment when the brain categorises a piece of knowledge differently, so that it becomes part of a different conceptual domain and creates a new knowledge structure. One of the most famous historic examples of a new knowledge structure being formed through an insight is that of Archimedes who invented a way to measure the volume of an irregularly shaped object.

Archimedes, born in Syracuse in the third century BC, was already considered a famous scholar during his lifetime. He practiced mathematics, physics and astronomy and invented numerous scientific laws and practical tools. Therefore, when King Hiero II of Syracuse doubted the quality of his golden laurel wreath, he considered Archimedes the right person to help him find out whether it was made from solid gold. Since, obviously, Archimedes wasn't allowed to melt down the crown, he couldn't change it into a shape of which the volume was easy to measure. But the volume was essential for determining the density of the crown and, eventually, whether or not it was made of solid gold. The volume was thus the important piece of the puzzle that was missing.

The seemingly impossible task troubled Archimedes for days. He rummaged through all the accumulated knowledge within the relevant conceptual domains. However, the solution couldn't be found in the conceptual domains he was turning upside down, because it was hidden in a seemingly irrelevant conceptual domain. The answer came at an unexpected moment, when Archimedes was taking a bath and noticed that the level of the water rose when he changed his position in the bath. In a split second, he realised that this effect was the key to determining the volume of the crown. He could submerge the crown in a cylinder, filled with water and with known dimensions, and measure the difference in water level. The amount of water displaced equalled the volume of the crown. Archimedes was so excited that he leapt from his bath and ran into the streets of Syracuse naked, crying *"Eureka!"* – in Greek meaning "I have found it!" The term 'eureka' is still used to describe this kind of aha-moment, and has become more famous than the anecdote itself.

When an insight enters our mind we basically see what everyone has seen before, but we think what no one else has thought – as Nobel laureate Albert Szent-Gyorgyi put it. As explained in chapter 1, this means that our perception classifies what we see into a new category. In Archimedes' case, the water level of the bath changing had been seen innumerable times, but it received a new meaning by imagining it in a cylinder as a way to measure the density of an irregular object.

Pleasure

Of course, insights that make all the pieces of the puzzle fall together and help the creative mind to see a hidden knowledge structure in its full glory don't just come to scientists. In the artistic domain, insights also occur constantly. After all, artists also give meaning to the world around them by building knowledge structures. In fact, most artists have a rich and uninhibited imagination to help them see what we all see, but think something different. The appreciation from the artist's audience might be slightly different, though. According to Arthur Koestler, there are three kinds of reactions to 'seeing' an insight. One includes an element of wisdom: "aha!" This is the classic eureka moment that was experienced by Archimedes. Then there's the type of insight the artistic domain often tries to evoke, which makes the audience go "ah…" Then, finally, there's the insight that contains an element of humour: "haha!" Of course, the division between the three is not very strict, since art uses humour, too, and science can provoke both admiration and laughter – when nobody believes a theory. However, the division at least indicates that creative insights come in different forms. What all these forms have in common is that they occur when a new knowledge structure is being formed that bridges different domains. Since our brain is designed to discern knowledge patterns and discover unfamiliar combinations, all of these insights are experienced as pleasurable, which is probably why the 'aha', 'ah', and 'haha' exclamations all sound like some sort of relief.

Finding without searching

Since insights are so important for creativity, it would be nice to be able to know when exactly we can expect them to occur. But we don't. However, we do know *where* they happen in the brain. When an insight occurs, the *anterior superior temporal gyrus* of the right hemisphere of our brain, located above the ear, lights up in a brain scan. We have two temporals, above both ears, but since the neurons in the right hemisphere are wired with wider branching, they can more easily source data and thus catch a missing piece of information. Which is one of the reasons why people always say that creativity happens in the right brain.

We can detect insights, but we still can't force them upon ourselves. That is why Picasso said: *"I never search, I find."* He understood that desperately searching for creativity couldn't force the insight to happen. Archimedes and Picasso were not the only ones who said that creativity just came to them effortlessly, as if offered by an external force. Mozart, too, said he just copied the music he heard in his mind, and Bob Dylan said about his songs that they came "through" him so that he didn't have to compose them. As early as thousands of years ago, it was believed that there is an invisible power that presents creativity on a silver platter. In Greek mythology, the Muses, the goddesses of literature and the arts, provide us with creative ideas. They were said to breathe original ideas into people, which causes someone to breathe 'aha.' This is why we say creativity is derived from 'inspiration,' which literally means to get breathed upon. As discussed in chapter 4, centuries later, in the second half of the 18th century, this idea still existed and fed the Romantic movement in believing that creativity was produced *entirely* by an irrational unconsciousness.

Preparation

Creativity is everything but an easy gain, offered on a silver platter. Before the insight happens, there is always a stage in the creative process that is called 'preparation.' During this stage we do research, collect information, assess related ideas, and listen to suggestions from others. This is a very rational, laborious, and often even frustrating part of the creative process, because no scientific, inventive, conceptual, or artistic results are booked. Archimedes extensively went through this stage before his insight occurred. He had been pondering a solution for days, gathering all the knowledge he needed to be able to theoretically solve the problem, and approaching it from as many different angles as possible. What was so important about this search is that the water level would have never featured as a solution without his preparation. In a way, it was at the 'tip of his brain.'

Archimedes' insight is a good example of an isolated problem, an isolated preparation stage, and an insight directly related to the problem. Since most creative minds are highly energetic and productive and work on many more or less related projects at the same time, what often happens is that the preparation for project A feeds into project B. Sometimes this happens with great lengths of time in between. The preparation stage can even take decades, since some creative minds dedicate their entire life to building a knowledge structure in one single conceptual domain by constantly gathering knowledge and learning more about this domain.

Galapagos finches

For example, in the 1830s, when Charles Darwin travelled around the cost of South America in the famous ship *HMS Beagle*, he didn't know he was going to create a theory that would explain how species are different from each other and change over time. Rather, he was simply commissioned to describe the plants and animals he would encounter on his trip. The voyage proved crucial for his theory, though. One of the species he described in his notebook were the various finches that lived on the different Galapagos Islands. Much later, he discovered, with the help of an ornithologist, that certain physical traits, such as the size and shape of the birds' beaks, were highly adapted to different food sources on the different islands where they lived. On one island the beaks were sturdy and short, adapted to cracking nuts, while on another island they were thin and long, adapted to picking food from crevices. Thus, while working on a commissioned project, he was already preparing for his famous evolution theory without knowing it. After his voyage, Darwin also spent some time studying barnacles and worms, which helped shape his evolution theory. That's why Darwin, a born naturalist, was preparing for insights to happen during most of his life.

Although Darwin had already written down all the important pieces of the puzzle that could form his evolution theory, the key insight for completing it came to him in 1838. The insight came from Thomas Malthus, who had published a work on the struggle for survival of ordinary people. After having read his work, Darwin suddenly realised how favourable variations would be preserved in this struggle of human beings, while unfavourable ones would be destroyed. After his 'Malthusian' insight, Darwin realised he finally had "a theory to work with."

Inspiration

While Darwin had been preparing his theory for many years already before the crucial insight occurred, it was not preparation but *inspiration* that offered it to him. The difference between the two sources of knowledge is that preparation happens in a specific conceptual domain and is aimed at solving a specific creative problem, while inspiration comes unexpectedly from sources that are acquired out of a general interest or even by coincidence – as happened in Archimedes' case as well.

Another example of inspiration is the trip British sculptor Henry Moore made when he was 26 and only at the beginning of his career. Moore travelled through Europe to study historical works of art. In Rome he studied Michelangelo and in Paris he encountered a Mayan *Chac Mool* statue, depicting a reclining human figure with its head up and facing the viewer. This shape strongly inspired him. Four years later, when he completed his first commissioned work, a relief at the headquarters of the London *Underground*, the influence of both Michelangelo's figures and the Chac Mool were clearly visible; they merged in his relief. Even decades later, in his more modern works, Moore kept using the reclining figure.

While both cases of inspiration demonstrate the difference between preparation and inspiration, they also show that the difference is almost merely semantic. After all, Moore went to Rome and Paris to study art and *prepare* for becoming an artist. He eventually used this preparatory work for being an artist. And although Darwin received his inspiration from a book about *human beings* – not the animals or plants he usually studied – it was no coincidence that the book was about the struggle for survival. You could therefore just as well say that we are always preparing for insights, even when we are absorbing knowledge from conceptual domains that are merely indirectly related to the creative projects we are working on.

9.

Unconscious Sensibility

It is by logic we prove,
it is by intuition that we invent.

Henri Poincaré

Bath, bus, bed

As Archimedes' example from the previous chapter clearly shows, the paradox of finding an insight is that only when we stop consciously searching for it, we'll come across it. The stage during which we are not consciously searching for a solution always follows the stage of preparation and is called 'incubation.' During incubation we take our focus off the creative process to let the knowledge we've gathered sink in, digest, and to let our unconscious brain organise it. This can take a very short time (a minute) or much longer (a sabbatical). Therefore, it's no coincidence that Archimedes' groundbreaking insight almost literally emerged from the water he was sitting in. It came to him when he was taking a bath, relaxing, thinking of something else. Psychologists often speak of the three B's when talking about places where insights are born; bath, bus, and bed. These are the places where the mind is at ease, not focused or strained, and has time to wander freely. It's at those moments that the mind diverges into unorthodox directions encountering pieces of information, not related to the conceptual domain one is working in, but essential for making unfamiliar combinations.

One of the very best moments for a mind to make new combinations is during a vacation, preferably in an exotic place. First of all, of course, because lying in a hammock relaxes us, which is thus comparable to one of the three B's. Secondly, because we encounter new cultural knowledge and experiences, which can be used as inspiration. Thirdly, because when we are in unexpected situations we receive all kinds of new stimuli that cannot be categorised by our perception the way we're used to, which forces our brain to create new categories. A positive side effect of leaving the well-travelled neural pathways to process the new experiences is that it becomes easier to abandon fixed assumptions and to categorise things differently. This is why Paul Simon's trip to South Africa to create Graceland was not just fruitful for an immersion in a completely different musical culture, but also for very subtly resetting his brain, in a way.

Creative process

The stage of incubation ends immediately when the unconscious brain connects with our conscious brain to share an insight. That's when the creative process turns conscious again, and proceeds onto the third stage, the verification stage. During this stage we evaluate the insight, check whether it matches with the available knowledge, elaborate on it, develop it, and polish it. In scientific domains, the verification stage is more theoretical, whereas in artistic domains the verification stage is more often physical, occupied as much by the message as by the medium.

Though the three-stage model of preparation, incubation, and verification is useful for understanding the importance of both our conscious and unconscious brain in the creative process, in reality there's mostly not such a clear distinction between the three stages. In every creative process – regardless of whether it takes days, months, or years – the borders between conscious and unconscious thinking are vague. The different parts of the brain responsible for the different stages constantly 'communicate' with each other and share and exchange information. Darwin, constructing his evolution theory, is a good example. As a true naturalist, Darwin was always observing the flora and fauna around him and consciously gathering information, and since the route to the completion of his theory was infested with small insights, he constantly switched back and forth in between the three stages. Thus, while in his autobiography he speaks of a clear epiphany that made all the pieces of the puzzle fall into place, most of the elements of his theory were already gathered in his mind and written down in his notebooks long before this specific insight.

The superior unconscious

The fact that incubation plays such an important role in the creative process feels somewhat counter-intuitive, because what distinguishes us on this planet as a species is a conscious mind that is able to process knowledge and form new and valuable ideas while being aware of it. The place in our brain where ideas are consciously formed is the *prefrontal cortex*, a tissue directly behind the forehead that vastly expanded as the human brain evolved and became more intelligent. The most important benefit to this large prefrontal cortex is a cognitive capacity called 'working memory.' Since, as discussed in chapter 1, our imagination sources from our memory, a bigger working memory increases the capacity to form new ideas. The information stored in this working – or short-term – memory can be attentively scanned, assessed, contemplated, and combined. The prefrontal cortex thus allows us to focus on specific thoughts, work towards a defined goal, concentrate on the present, and ignore all the irrelevant thoughts that cross our mind.

Despite the unique character of our consciousness, our unconscious is the smartest part of our brain. When it comes to processing data, for example, our unconscious is superior. When we are consciously writing, reading, or counting, for example, we can process a mere maximum of 60 bits of data per second – which is why, for example, we're so bad at multi-tasking. However, the *unconscious* processing power of all the receptors of our senses combined – seeing, hearing, smelling, tasting, and feeling – is estimated to be over 10 million bits of data per second.

This is what enables us to make a judgement about someone we see for the very first time in milliseconds. Our unconscious mind has already 'sensed' that someone is a bit sloppy well before our conscious mind notices that he is wearing two different socks, has cut himself with the razor, or has a tiny coffee stain on his shirt. The ability of our unconscious brain to quickly scan data also helps us filter the overload of information that is constantly fired at us. If our conscious mind, with its limited capacity, would have to deal with all the sensory input relevant for our many different creative projects, it would become overloaded.

You could say that the filtering qualities of our unconscious brain makes the life of a creative mind bearable. However, the irony of the importance of filtering information is that creative minds are not very good at this. This is why creative minds have a bigger chance of being bipolar or schizophrenic. People with these diseases have a hard time in separating important stimuli from less important stimuli, which makes them easily distracted and hyper-associative. The upside to this chaotic personality is that it helps to more easily make combinations of relevant and irrelevant information.

Intuition

The unconscious mind doesn't just help us with filtering data; it even assists in making decisions. Again, our unconscious mind is usually much better at this than our conscious mind. The decisive power of our unconscious mind can be compared to the qualities of an expert chess player who can perform very effectively at a rate of one move every 5 to 10 seconds. Many digital multiplayer role-playing games even require a faster decision speed, though the decisions might be less complex. At that kind of decision-making speed there's no time for extensive analysis or comparison of different moves. It's the unconscious mind that oversees the game and makes the decisions. In the creative process these unconscious decisions separate the good ideas that are formed in our mind from the bad ones, regardless of whether it's simply a move in the game or pursuing a new scientific theory. As creative minds generate many new ideas – both consciously and unconsciously – there needs to be some sort of sieve that filters out which ideas are worth pursuing and which are not. The secret to having good ideas is simply having many ideas and throwing away the bad ones, according to Nobel Laureate Linus Pauling. Or as one of the creators of the animated sitcom South Park, Matt Stone, put it: *"For all the good ideas there's like 100 not so good ones."* This implies that saying 'no' is at least as important as relentlessly pursuing an idea. After all, if you spend too much time finding out that your idea is useless – or, in technical terms, 'invaluable' – you are wasting your time.

Making decisions unconsciously is also called intuition. What's interesting about intuition is that it actually follows the knowledge patterns that were established during the conscious stages of the creative process. All the technical and cultural knowledge we gathered consciously is thus taken into account when our intuition is telling us we're making the right decision. So, intuition is based on knowledge, and that's exactly why the more experienced you are in a certain creative domain, the easier it is to trust your intuition in separating the bad ideas from the good ones. However, as we've established in chapter 5, too much experience is not helpful either, since the 'groves' in the patterns of knowledge in our neural network then become too deep and inflexible. Since the well-trodden networks in our white matter are too easy for the brain to follow, fewer unexpected combinations will be made and passed on to our consciousness.

Mind-wandering

The reason that unconscious insights have more creative potential than conscious insights, generated in our prefrontal cortex, is that our unconscious brain, located in the right hemisphere of the brain, has the ability to make remote associations. A *remote* association is what separates an obvious insight from a truly surprising one. Scientists still don't know exactly what happens in our brain when we make remote associations, but it is believed that both relevant and seemingly irrelevant – or 'remote' – information constantly moves through our brain at a high speed and is quickly combined in many different ways. Some say these combinations are formed more or less blindly and some say they are made along the lines of simple associations. In the latter case, our brain combines different pieces of information that were once linked – however brief, indirect or superficial – in our mind.

The randomness of remote associations can be compared to dreaming; our dreams also trigger and combine memories and associations that we have consciously gathered when awake, either recently or a long time ago. Since this happens in an arbitrary way it generates surreal stories. The theory that dreaming is in some way related to the remote associations of our unconscious brain is reinforced by the fact that mind-wandering is a kind of temporary and light sleep mode – also called daydreaming – which turns down the activity in the prefrontal cortex, so that we lose attention for the external world and turn inward. We actually even literally turn inward since our visual cortex also partly shuts down, so that we only partly register what happens in front of our eyes – even when they are open. When our mind is wandering we are better able to source from remote knowledge and come up with unexpected combinations. It is even the case that people who easily engage in mind-wandering score significantly higher on measures of creativity. If it's not in your nature to easily tap into your remote knowledge, mind-wandering can also be induced by tasks that require little conscious attention such as walking, driving a car or even reading a tedious book.

Beautiful ideas

The next question to ask, then, is how our unconscious mind knows it has stumbled upon an insight that is worth passing on to the conscious mind. In the beginning of the 20th century, the French mathematician, scientist, and philosopher Henri Poincaré introduced the term 'aesthetic sensibility' to explain how the ideas with potential are separated from the useless ones. To incorporate aesthetics into creative process seems misleading. Though nature produces forms that are generally considered beautiful, since our minds have adjusted to them through evolution, in the man-made world beauty is usually in the eye of the beholder. Or, from a sociocultural point of view, beauty is at least culturally biased. When Duchamp put a urinal upside down, it earned a prominent place in the history of art because it was conceptually groundbreaking, not for being beautiful.

Another reason why 'aesthetic' seems the wrong term for assessing the value of an idea is that the meaning is more easily associated with art, music, and poetry, rather than with science. This is why, according to Poincaré, aesthetic sensibility should be understood as harmonious, elegant, and well-proportioned. You could also say, as Immanuel Kant did, that the ultimate beauty is found in truth and order. That is probably what Mendeleyev experienced when he conceived the Periodic Table; it must have seemed to contain truth and order since every known chemical element was captured in the model. Our unconscious thus assists us not literally in finding beautiful ideas, but in finding ideas that beautifully fit in an existing body of knowledge. Thus, you could say that while the conscious mind aims to rearrange our knowledge, the unconsciousness mind somewhat paradoxically makes sure it is rearranged harmoniously.

10.

Evolution Explores

*If we don't get lost,
we'll never find a new route*

Joan Littlewood

Tiger shark wanted

Though we need to heavily rely on our unconscious brain for the greatest ideas to pop up, the biggest part of the creative process consists of the conscious stages of preparation and verification. What's more, however bright the idea that pops into our mind is, converting it into a physical form proves much more difficult than you might imagine. That's why the creative path is often paved with problems, and all of these problems require extra preparation and verification. Simply put, most of the creative process is hard work. Thomas Edison, with over a 1,000 patents in his name one of the greatest inventors that ever lived, aptly summarised the creative process as: '1% is inspiration, 99% is perspiration.'

A famous piece of art that reflects the difference between inspiration and perspiration is Damien Hirst's *The Physical Impossibility of Death in the Mind of Someone Living*; a real – but dead – shark displayed in a huge, blue-glassed, liquid-filled vitrine, suggesting that the shark is displayed in his natural habitat. The idea of making a dead shark look alive and provoking fear among its audience was easily conceived of. However, building it proved quite difficult. At first, Hirst wanted to use the most fearful of all sharks, the great white. It was Steven Spielberg that had inspired him with the movie *Jaws*, which he had watched as a child. But just before he tried to buy a great white in Australia, the species was declared protected. Therefore, he needed to settle for a smaller shark – or, rather, not as huge: the tiger shark. He then discovered that buying a shark in Australia wasn't exactly easy. Where to start? As there was no internet at the time, Hirst called all the local post offices in an area in Australia known for harbouring tiger sharks. He asked them to put up a sign saying *"Tiger shark wanted."* After he found one – people were calling him in the middle of the night to offer him sharks – he shipped it to England and prepared it with formaldehyde to preserve it, which was quite some work. He also needed to build a container that could hold the liquid and the shark, and a way to suspend the shark in the container. When he finally finished, he found out that the shark wasn't properly conserved; it started to decay and the liquid in the container quickly grew murky. Hirst tried to solve this problem by completely gutting the shark and stretching its skin over a fibreglass mould. Subsequently, the next problem occurred; the mould instantly made the shark look fake, incapable of provoking fear. This thus killed the soul of the whole concept. To solve this problem, a new tiger shark was caught in Australia, shipped to England, and this time subjected to a $100,000 formaldehyde process, supervised by a scientist and a curator of the *American Museum of Natural History* in New York. Only then was it ready for display.

What's ironic about the process of making Hirst's shark is that, as a conceptual artist, Hirst believes that an idea can exist without its physical body, and thus solely in the mind of the creator. In other words, the intention is enough. In a way, he is right, because if you see the shark today, it looks quite dead and anything but frightening. However, if the mere intention would be enough, another one of Hirst's ideas – showing a real rainbow in a gallery – could already become *historically* creative, simply by sharing it. The complicated process of bringing it into existence and proving that it's possible in real life could then simply be skipped. However, as we've learned in chapter 2, without a medium the idea can't be experienced, nor valued by an audience. Especially in the artistic domain, the experience is essential. Therefore, without actually creating it, Hirst's rainbow is just another idea. Even Sol LeWitt, who merely wrote down the instructions for his artworks for others to execute them in order to prove that the appearance of a work was secondary to the idea, had his ideas turned into a medium.

Happy accidents

The entire creative process can be compared to exploring a map that is still partly undiscovered. Some important places and connecting roads are missing, and the process of exploration is essential for making the map complete. A classic example of the importance of exploration for finding new ways is Christopher Columbus discovering America in 1492; if he hadn't tried to land on the East Indies going West instead of East, his discovery might not have been made. With the knowledge available, he should have indeed arrived at the East Indies, but instead he found a huge area on the map; an entire continent between Europe and the East Indies.

Each route that is tried out in the creative process, even a dead end, teaches something that further expands the knowledge structure, makes it more detailed, and brings the complete picture a little closer. And only when the map is complete, can the most efficient route become visible. Which is why in hindsight the solution always seems obvious. Or, as Einstein put it: *"In light of knowledge attained, the happy achievement seems almost a matter of course."*

Though creative exploration is often experienced to be frustrating, it helps to shape the initial idea and often improves it. The inspiration for Hirst's work, Steven Spielberg's *Jaws*, which came out in 1975 was strongly influenced by a highly challenging production. The novel by Peter Benchley, upon which the movie was quite faithfully based, already existed, but the construction of the prop sharks required 40 technicians. Operating and filming the mechanical sharks proved a disaster; they malfunctioned, absorbed water, sank, and broke constantly. Instead of the scheduled 65 days, it took 157 days to make the movie and instead of the budgeted $4 million, the movie ended up costing $9 million. However, the unreliability of the shark proved a blessing in disguise, since Steven Spielberg was forced to shoot most of the scenes with the shark by only hinting at it – for example, by simply filming the water level, the shark's dorsal fin or a set of floating barrels that were supposedly attached to it. According to Spielberg, this suggestive approach – inspired by Alfred Hitchcock – only increased the suspense of the movie and contributed to its huge success. If the entire process of making the movie had gone as smoothly as *Universal Pictures* had imagined it, it would have been a different movie and maybe not as successful. Instead, it became the very first blockbuster, grossing the highest amount ever up until then.

Exploration does not just present new, surprising routes, but sometimes the accidents in a creative process show an entirely new conceptual map. In the scientific world, there are many examples of these kinds of happy accidents. To name a few, this was how Alexander Fleming, Wilhelm Röntgen, and Louis Daguerre became world-famous. They invented the daguerreotype in 1839 (the forerunner of modern photography), the X-Ray in 1895, and penicillin in 1928, respectively. In Daguerre's case, it was due to a spilled jar of mercury in a cabinet in which he stored silver plates, after which the mercury produced a perfect image on the plates. Röntgen was doing experiments with vacuum tubes when he accidentally discovered a fluorescent effect, caused by the 'X-Ray,' on a piece of cardboard that was only there to protect an aluminium window. In Fleming's case, it was mould that accidentally infiltrated his lab through an open window.

Trial and error

The less a conceptual domain has been discovered or, more specifically, the less knowledge one possesses of a conceptual domain, the more routes one needs to explore to create something new. In other words, when you are as blind as the man searching for the black hat in chapter 8, trial and error becomes a more important part of the creative process. The inventor Charles Goodyear, for example, heavily relied on trial and error in the process of discovering vulcanised rubber in 1839. The vulcanisation of rubber was an important invention, because natural, uncured rubber is sticky, deforms easily when warm, and is brittle when cold. On an atomic level the vulcanisation of rubber was meant to cross-link the long polymer chains, preventing them from moving separately, causing its stickiness. The vulcanisation would thus make the rubber stronger and at the same time give it its elastic qualities.

Unlike Watson and Crick, who were also searching for the cross-connection between polymers in our DNA, Charles Goodyear didn't approach the problem as a theoretical puzzle on an atomic level. Instead, he simply tried to treat the rubber with as many different chemicals as possible; it is said he even tried cream cheese. Many of his attempts were thus fairly random. After many years, however, he did successfully find out that sulphur would solve the problem of rubber's unsteady form. Goodyear's lengthy creative process resembled that of Edison in inventing the light bulb, which required as many as thousands of different experiments – *every failure told me something that I was able to incorporate into the next attempts.*" Just as Edison's light bulb, Goodyear's invention was one of great importance for the industrial revolution, especially since it made inflatable tires possible. That's how it inspired the company which started to produce rubber tires for

Henry Ford in the beginning of the 20th century to do so under Goodyear's name.

The extent of trial and error does not just depend on how well-discovered a domain is, but also on the rigidity of the domain and how well a problem is defined. Some creative minds prefer to work with ill-defined problems in a flexible domain because it allows them to do a lot of research and experiments and freely wander on an empty map. Some, however, are more goal-directed creative minds that prefer a more convergent creative process. This is the difference between a writer who writes a book in a single sitting, and one that works on a single book for a great part of his life. Personal factors that can decrease or increase the amount of trial and error are whether one is a doer or a thinker, self-confident or self-reflective, intuitive or rational, and nonchalant or perfectionistic.

Molecular gastronomy

An example of a perfectionist who gives himself lots of room to explore is the Spanish chef Ferran Adrià. He used to close his restaurant *El Bulli* for 6 months each year to extensively research ways to renew his menu. Though the eventual output – the dishes as presented to the customers – were small works of art, it was no coincidence that his cuisine was dubbed *molecular gastronomy*; his workshop resembled a scientific lab. By means of extensive trial and error, Adrià and his assistants combined ingredients in ways never conceived of before. Their exploration would start with treating different ingredients using different methods, such as steaming, cooking, frying, roasting, juicing, drying and vacuuming them. After they had studied how the ingredients changed colour, appearance, texture, smell, and taste, they would photograph the results, write down their findings, and give each preparation a mark. Subsequently, through a process of singling out the best ingredients, the best preparation, and the best combinations, the dishes were finally compiled. Even though Adrià's conceptual domain is primarily restricted by the senses, which makes it personal and subjective, the explorative process was quite methodical.

Many artists, whose creative processes are primarily ruled by intuitive decisions, have a studio that looks like the opposite of a scientific lab. Just like the Romantics from the previous chapter, they will tell you the answers simply come to them. Just like Picasso, who never searched but simply found. However, even Picasso used trial and error in his creative process and was sometimes more methodical than he would have liked to admit. For one of his most famous works *Guernica*, depicting the horrors of the bombing of the town of Guernica during the Spanish civil war, he made numerous sketches. A study of these sketches has revealed that he explored a myriad of possible figures and their configurations and how many of these explorations resulted in dead ends. The study also shows that the final figures in the painting often showed a greater resemblance to the earlier sketches than the later ones, which indicates that Picasso needed the dead ends to find the confirmation that his aesthetic sensibility led him to the right choice right from the start. But this process of exploration does not just have a confirmatory purpose. As in Spielberg's production, it shapes and often improves the initial idea.

Natural selection

The importance of trial and error in creating something new and valuable has a striking analogy with Charles Darwin's evolution theory. Darwin's theory on natural selection can be brought down to two elements: blind variation and selective retention. The first element, blind variation, explains that each member of a population is randomly different. The second element, selective retention, explains that the differences that suit a changing environment are retained. Thus the finches from chapter 8 that Darwin studied when he was on the Galapagos Islands were randomly born with different beaks. However, the birds with beaks that were useful for finding and eating the food on their specific island survived and became a subspecies.

The Darwinian blind variation and selective retention also takes place in our unconscious brain which more or less randomly combines information and uses our aesthetic sensibility to forward the ideas deemed 'fit' to make it to the real world. When we zoom out a little, the real world shows us creative individuals such as Hirst, Spielberg, Adrià, and Picasso who consciously try and fail to slowly shape their ideas into a physical work. When we zoom out a bit more, on a cultural level, a selection also takes place among the ideas that are presented to the domain. This way, a culture also slowly adapts to its environment and dies out when it isn't able to. Therefore, at every level in the creative process – the cerebral, individual, and cultural level – trial and error plays an important role. Different from Darwin's trial and error, though, is that our creative efforts are never completely blind. Our trials – both consciously and unconsciously – always have direction and are based on the conceptual knowledge structures in our minds.

11.

Connected Visions

*Every man takes the limits
of his own field of vision
for the limits of the world*

Arthur Schopenhauer

Notebook

We know now that creativity is not just about the 'aha' moment, but usually involves a lengthy, arduous process of exploration. For instance, take Charles Darwin's book *On the Origin of Species*, published in 1859, in which he explains his famous theory. 28 years before the book was published, Darwin left on his five-year adventure around the world during which he laid the basis for his theory. Then in 1838, about two years after his return, he came to his crucial insight on the struggle for survival, as described in chapter 8. But only 21 years after this insight, his book was finished. Darwin's book is a good example of how conceptual domains, and the ideas built on them, often reach their maturity very slowly.

To connect all his studies and findings along the way, Darwin used a notebook. In this notebook he didn't just write down his observations and draw the species he encountered, but also played with ideas and generally let his mind wander on the page. You could say that his notebook worked as an extension of his prefrontal cortex. After all, as explained in chapter 9, that is the place in our brain where we consciously combine, analyse and weigh different ideas. But since the working memory in our prefrontal cortex can only store a limited amount of information and fleeting ideas sometimes pass through it very quickly, we can effectively extend the capacity of our working memory by making notes of our explorations. In doing so, the notebook becomes a space where our conscious brain interacts with our past observations and where ideas can be cultivated and grow. Especially in the more analytical creative domains, keeping a notebook can easily expand our prefrontal cortex and thus the amount of conscious combinations we can make.

World wide web

The sophistication of the notebook has strongly improved thanks to the introduction of the *digital* 'notebook'. Due to the ever-evolving software, today our notebooks are not just good for taking notes anymore, they can even help us to imagine complex 3D models. An even bigger leap in the capacity of our notebook is the invention of the internet; the amounts of knowledge coming from this source form a virtual extension of our notebook with almost unlimited capacity. That's why the internet is an invention at least as revolutionary as that of the printing press; both have dramatically democratised the access to knowledge. Though not all knowledge on the internet is directly useful, we at least have it at our fingertips in our modern-day notebook.

Access to more knowledge is so important for creativity because, as explained in chapter 5, knowledge forms the basis of all creativity. What makes the internet a much bigger revolution than the printing press is that it's a dynamic source of knowledge that constantly grows, changes, and adapts, and is more easily accessible because we can all contribute to it. The most obvious example is *Wikipedia*: anyone with a special interest in a specific (niche) subject – amateur or professional – can create a lemma on it or edit one. And, in addition to the great amount of knowledge it holds, the internet is also interactive, so that it enables people to build knowledge structures in collaboration.

Just like the completion of Darwin's theory, the invention of the world wide web in 1990 was also a lengthy process. According to the founding father of the internet, Tim Berners-Lee, there wasn't even a 'eureka' moment involved; it was a process of 'accretion' (read: gradual growth). The very first source for Berners-Lee's idea was also a book that collected an enormous amount of information. Not a notebook, but a very old Victorian encyclopaedia, called *Enquire Within Upon Everything*, lying around his parents' house when he was a child. He was so fond of the book and fascinated by the possibility to explore such a wide range of unrelated, random information that it planted a seed of inspiration in him. During his professional life, Berners-Lee worked at a telecommunications company, a software company helping computers to form networks, and finally at the European nuclear research lab *CERN*, where he built a hypertext-based prototype tool that facilitated sharing and updating information among researchers – basically the predecessor of the internet. All the knowledge, experience, and skills Berners-Lee gathered during his life thus slowly but surely built the internet.

Global city

When we look at the amount and variety of knowledge on the internet, there are parallels with the most creative cities throughout history, such as Athens in the fifth century BC, the Arab cities in the tenth century, Florence during the high Renaissance, Venice in the fifteenth century, Paris, London, and Vienna in the nineteenth century, and New York in the twentieth century. What these cultural capitals have in common is that they were affluent, entrepreneurial, and functioned as international trade hubs, which meant they inhabited many subcultures, each with their own specialised knowledge and conceptual domains. These cities were thus home to complex networks of knowledge. But it's not just the wealth of knowledge that made these cities such creative places. It was also the scale and density of the population that increased the chance of subcultures – which wouldn't naturally be drawn to each other – colliding, interacting, and combining their knowledge. This effect also occurs in smaller communities where large amounts of knowledge and people with different backgrounds flock together such as Silicon Valley and universities, for instance.

The most important differences between the internet and these cities are that the world wide web is a global city, as it were, unhindered by distances and borders, with much more knowledge and possibilities to connect. Each person can connect to any other person on the internet relatively easily. This is actually what makes our brain such an effective creative machine; the 100 million neurons inside the brain can also very easily communicate with each other – the average neuron transmits signals to about a thousand other neurons. However, what makes our global city more efficient than our brain is that we can actively follow, share and discuss knowledge in a very directed manner. Even though, as we've seen with regard to our brain's white matter described in chapter 7, more efficiency decreases the number of serendipitous collisions, it does make the creative process more effective. And since our global 'digital city' will only carry more social connections, sensors, data, knowledge, and intelligence, its creative potential will only grow.

Brainstorming

When we zoom in on a creative connection between two individuals, the potential of this connection to stimulate and improve the creative process lies in the fact that they enrich each other with unexpected angles and views and complement each other's knowledge gaps. A simple example of how we can become complementary to each other in this respect is the discovery of the structure of our DNA. Rosalind Franklin was also trying to discover the DNA structure. She primarily used X-Ray crystallography and hoped that the data from the images would enable her to *see* the structure. But Franklin's X-Ray technology at that time was still in its infancy and couldn't give an accurate view of the complete structure. However, it was Franklin's X-Ray data that made the helical structure visible, which proved a crucial piece in Watson and Crick's puzzle. And along with Franklin's piece of knowledge, there were several other theoretical pieces used in the final structure. These pieces came from different scientific domains, such as biochemistry, genetics, information theory, and mathematics. Since Watson and Crick didn't master all of these domains, they needed to connect to others to build their theory.

Sharing knowledge is important, but having an active conversation even catalyses the creative process. The reason for this is that discussing an idea with someone else enables the creative mind to look at its own idea through someone else's eyes. In a way, it makes two or more brains become one and thus generates a richer, more adaptive, reflective, and eventually more effective creative process. So while the interaction with Franklin was very limited – her data were even shared without her knowledge – Watson and Crick were known to have long coffee breaks together during which they intensely exchanged ideas. These mini-brainstorms were especially fruitful because of their different scientific backgrounds, Watson being a geneticist and Crick a biophysicist. It made their creative potential bigger than the sum of their parts.

In the artistic domain, the creative process is catalysed in the same manner. As described in chapter 6, Paul Simon's successful album Graceland was also a product of interaction. Not always verbally, as musical instruments speak a language of their own, but especially through lengthy jamming sessions – the musical equivalent of brainstorming – with Simon's pop music on the one hand and the South Africans with their Zulu genres on the other. Of course, this is only a fairly simple example of a creative collaboration. Today, the most popular creative products, such as television, films, shows, music videos, computer software, and video games are collaborations based on a relatively complex network of skilled individuals. As the amount of knowledge, tools, skills, and conceptual subdomains is constantly expanding and becomes more specialised, creative collaborations and efficient ways of communicating and sharing knowledge become increasingly important.

Single-minded vision

An important weakness of creative collaborations is that for a group it's extremely difficult to come up with a focused and single-minded idea. In fact, the bigger the group, the more difficult this is. Even in bands there are usually one or two individuals that create most of the music. The obvious benefit to a group is that it has a bigger combined prefrontal cortex in the conscious preparation and verification stages, helping to build knowledge structures, brainstorming, evaluating ideas and elaborating on them. However, eventually an insight happens in one single brain, not in a couple. What's more, most groups don't have the intrinsic motivation and single-minded vision of a creative individual. That's why statues are never built for committees, as each member of a committee has a different motivation and vision. Even Wikipedia, an often-used example of a creative collaboration, was conceived by just two individuals, Jimmy Wales and Larry Sanger. They came up with the idea to build a free online encyclopaedia, *not* the crowd submitting and editing lemmas.

Collaborative creativity has become especially useful in executing complex ideas, such as building skyscrapers and creating blockbusters. The reason for this is that complex ideas require distributed cognition, which means that each member of the team contributes a unique and essential piece to the end product. Director Stanley Kubrick, for example, couldn't have made 2001; A Space Odyssey on his own. Though the idea to make a science fiction film based on the book *The Sentinel*, written by Arthur C. Clarke, came from Kubrick alone, he hired a very specialised set of people to 'physically' create the film. Among them was Clarke himself, who wrote the screenplay, a production designer, a special effects specialist, and a composer. All these specialists were responsible for an essential part of the movie, but it was Kubrick who aligned them with his vision and who gave the creative process direction accordingly.

Steve Jobs

The more commercial a creative production becomes, the harder it is to align all parties involved. The most important reason for this is that commercial leaders have different objectives than artistic leaders, which per definition makes a single-minded view impossible. That's why big corporations can only become creative when there is a strong leader with a creative vision and clear sense of direction. Steve Jobs was such a leader. His single-minded vision was quite simple; making intuitive consumer electronics. The unfamiliar combination that made it creative was that it combined the geeky technology from Silicon Valley with a user-friendly experience by focusing on simplicity and design. With that vision in mind, he redefined the computer (into the *Macintosh*), portable music (into the *iPod*), the mobile phone (into the *iPhone*), and the business model of the music industry (into *iTunes*).

Though Jobs is known for his autocratic method of making decisions, he did understand the importance of creative collaboration. He believed in spontaneous meetings and was known for taking long walks with people he could learn from – even if they had dissenting views. When Jobs led *Pixar* in the late 90s, he designed the office in such a way that his employees would constantly run into each other in the atrium, stimulating seren-dipitous encounters. He also believed that 'deep collaboration' in the execution phase was essential to producing the seamless and intuitive Apple products in which software and hardware were optimally integrated. At Apple all specialised parties, such as designers, product developers, engineers, and manufactur-ers, were constantly involved in the creative process. It made the process uniquely concurrent, instead of sequential. However, the most important building block for Apple's success was Jobs himself, who was the undisputed leader, not afraid to step on toes, and uncompromisingly sent products back to the drawing board if they didn't comply with his vision.

Changing the universe

So, the final paradox in this book is that, while creativity thrives when individuals are connected and actively share knowledge, skills, and ideas, the creative process always requires a single-minded idea that is executed with a single-minded vision. Even when our planet has become a digitally connected meta-brain that interacts by itself – similarly to the prebiotic chemistry on our planet that slowly created intelligent life – we will always need creative minds with God-like aspirations that have a clear vision of how to change the universe – or maybe, at some point, how to create an entirely new one.

Creativity Defined

Creativity seems indefinable because, as this book demonstrates, it can be approached on different levels and from different angles. It is therefore impossible to capture creativity in one single definition. However, that doesn't mean that it cannot be defined. Here are the most important definitions that can be distilled from this book.

Innovation – Chapter 1
Creativity builds entirely new ideas using existing virtual and physical building blocks.

Imagination – Chapters 1, 6 and 8
Creativity uses imagination to perceive that which we see and already know in new ways.

Discovery – Chapters 1 and 10
Creativity makes visible that which was invisible before.

Communication – Chapters 1 and 2
Creativity brings ideas into existence by turning them into communicable forms, such as work of arts, performances, inventions, and written theories, so that they can be shared with an audience.

World-view – Chapters 2 and 6
Creativity is a new – objective or subjective – view on the world.

Everyone – Chapters 2 and 7
Creativity is based on a variety of cognitive and unconscious abilities that we all posses to a greater or lesser extent.

Culture – Chapters 2 and 3
Creativity is a sociocultural mechanism that only allows new ideas to enter a creative domain when they are considered valuable.

Change – Chapters 3 and 5
Creativity changes the technical and cultural rules that define a creative domain.

Motivation – Chapter 4
Creativity is a psychological motivator that helps creators to focus on making their ideas become reality.

 Creativity Defined

Happiness – Chapter 4

Creativity makes people happy when they are fully occupied with it, not thinking about anything that is irrelevant to the creative process.

Combination – Chapters 6, 8 and 9

Creativity combines familiar knowledge, from a specific conceptual domain, with seemingly irrelevant knowledge, from another domain, to make an unfamiliar combination.

Problem-finding – Chapter 7

Creativity finds problems by questioning the existing knowledge structure of a conceptual domain.

Problem-solving – Chapter 7

Creativity is a mental tool that solves problems by divergent thinking (finding as many solutions as possible) and convergent thinking (finding the best solution).

Insight – Chapters 8 and 9

Creativity unconsciously produces problem-solving insights that make new knowledge structures visible.

Process – Chapters 8 and 9

Creativity is a process that consists of internalizing the rules that define a domain ('preparation'), of letting the acquired knowledge digest while we wait for an insight to appear ('incubation'), and of assessing and executing the insight ('verification').

Harmony – Chapter 9

Creativity rearranges knowledge in a harmonious way.

Exploration – Chapter 10

Creativity shapes ideas by exploring different ways to execute them.

Evolution – Chapter 10
Creativity is an evolutionary mechanism of trial and error that helps human beings and cultures to constantly adapt to changing environments.

Interaction – Chapter 11
Creativity builds rich knowledge structures and executes complex ideas through interaction between individuals.

Any definition missing or any contributions you'd like to make? Please leave a message at www.definingcreativity.com.

Thanks

Among the many quotes on creativity I have collected during the process of writing *Defining Creativity,* there was one that I especially liked. It was Isaac Newton's famous expression: *"If I have seen further than other men it is because I have stood on the shoulders of giants."* Though, unlike Newton, I haven't seen much further than other men, I have definitely been using many shoulders over the past few years. Not just of the giants mentioned under Sources, but also the somewhat smaller shoulders of the proofreaders of this book. Due to their critical feedback I was able to see the book through different pairs of eyes and reflect on incorrect and incomplete details, to which I would otherwise have remained blind.

I therefore want to express my gratitude to the following people – in alphabetical order; Diederik Boon (physician), Sarina Bouwhuis (the editor of this book), Michael Floor (photographer), Jarr Geerligs (art director), Mariken van Himbergen (copywriter), Okke Hora Adema (industrial designer), William Pen (digital strategist), Graziëlla Piras (psychiatrist), Fleur Roos Rosa de Carvalho (curator), Mischa Rozema (director), Eddy Steeneken (musician), Garech Stone (creative director), Monique Voet (neurobiologist), and Rudolf van Wezel (the publisher of this book).

I also want to thank Hans van der Baan, who was responsible for the layout and distinctive colour of this book. Finally, a very special thanks to Rick de Zwart, who is responsible for the cover, the illustrations, and custom-made typefaces. It is always a great pleasure working with Rick. Not just because of his creativity and craftsmanship, but also due to his modesty and punctuality.

Amsterdam, 29 November 2013

Thanks

Sources

All the sources listed below have contributed to *Defining Creativity*. Since many of these sources show overlap in the most basic knowledge on creativity (e.g. the importance of including 'novelty' in the definition of creativity), it is not always clear exactly which source has contributed to which part of the book. However, for the cases in which it is known, this is mentioned underneath the source.

Books on creativity

Boden, Margaret A. (2004)
The Creative Mind: Myths and Mechanisms
This book describes the creation 'ex nihilo,' the example of the impressionist painting rejected by official exhibitions, the importance of the element

*of surprise when making creative combinations, the importance of prepa-
ration, the manner in which creativity is grounded in everyday abilities,
the analogy of exploring a conceptual space on a map that is still partly
undiscovered, the meaning of beauty for scientists, personal versus historical creativity, and the importance of the unconscious stage in the creative process.*

Berns, Gregory (2010)

Iconoclast: A Neuroscientist Reveals How to Think Differently

*This book discusses how imagination works, the difference between vision
and perception (how perception is about categorising what we see), the
efficiency of the brain (how what we perceive matches with what we've
seen before), the difficulty of imagining new visions, our natural fear of
the unknown and social embarrassment, the 'social' differences between
Van Gogh and Picasso, and some benefits of different drugs.*

Csikszentmihalyi, Mihaly (2009)

Creativity: Flow and the Psychology of Discovery and Invention

*This book explores the parallel between biological genes and cultural
memes, the different personality traits of creative individuals, the history
of IQ and creativity tests, how intuition works, the difference between
divergent and convergent thinking, the relation between the rigidity of a
domain and the creative peak age, the evolutionary merits of creativity,
the importance of having many ideas (using Linus Pauling's quote), talent
in relation to knowledge, the meaning of a domain in relation to a culture,
children's non-creativity, creative environments (such Florence in the Renaissance), and, as the title suggests, the meaning of flow.*

Johnson, Steven (2010)

Where Good Ideas Come From

This book describes the first chemical reactions slowly forming life on earth, the continuum between nature's and man-made creations, the 'slow hunch,' the principle of 'tinkering' (the invention of the printing press), Darwin's notebook and his 'Malthusian epiphany,' the importance of serendipity, the invention of the internet by Tim Berners-Lee, the importance of interaction, and more specifically the parallel between the internet, creative cities, and our brain.

Koestler, Arthur (1990)
The Act of Creation
This book discusses the chimpanzee using a stick to reach fruit outside her cage, the game of chess having limited creative possibilities, different kinds of insights ('aha,' 'haha,' and 'ah'), and discovery with our imagination.

Krausz, Michael; Dutton, Dennis; Bardsley, Karen (2009)
The Idea of Creativity
This book describes Karl Popper's metaphor of the blind man searching for a black hat, how creative people are more easily distracted, what a medium is, Darwin's blind-variation, selective-retention model in relation to creativity (along with the 'BVSR' examples of Picasso's Guernica and Goodyear's discovery of vulcanised rubber), Sol LeWitt's conceptual art, and Poincaré's 'aesthetic sensibility.'

Lehrer, Jonah (2010)
Imagine: How Creativity Works
This book examines the difference between our brain halves when it comes to seeing the bigger picture and details, how dopamine in our prefrontal cortex and drugs help us to pay attention and focus (using the example of Kerouac writing 'On the road'), how our (positive) mood influences creativity (e.g. happiness and solving puzzles), how dreaming and daydreaming influence creativity, why creative minds are more often bipolar, and the importance of interactivity in the creative process (using the example of how Steve Jobs designed the Pixar Studio).

Runco, Mark A. and Pritzker, Steven (2011)
Encyclopaedia of Creativity
This 2-volume encyclopaedia – which has collected almost all (scientific) knowledge on creativity available – was used for double-checking information or when needing a more elaborative explanation of certain topics. It discusses intrinsic versus extrinsic motivation and creative personalities, the definition of discovery according to Albert Szent-Gyorgyi, examples of scientists making discoveries by accident, divergent and convergent thinking, ill-defined and well-defined problems, the example of the increase of knowledge (using the example of the journal of science in 1670), the meaning of beauty (Kant: finding truth and order), the importance of filtering stimuli, and how creativity can help regulate emotions.

Sawyer, Keith R. (2006)
Explaining Creativity: The Science of Human Invention
This book explores the sociocultural perspective on creativity (Duchamp's Fountain), the role of the gatekeeper, the inverted-U learning curve, the different creative career peaks of Van Gogh and Cézanne, the Western versus the primitive/collectivist view on creativity, the Renaissance artists starting to sign their works, the psychological studies on creativity starting in the 1950s, the Romantic view on creativity, how creativity uses everyday cognitive processes (and the example of the size of Einstein's brain), the differences between the left and the right brain half, and distributed cognition.

Sternberg, Robert J. (2004)
Creativity: From Potential to Realization
This book discusses the meaning of value, how creative minds became celebrities in the 16th century, how creativity today is still linked to eccentricity (Jackson Pollock), the manner in which certain personality traits are linked to creativity, how cognitive talents work, the importance of being fluent in multiple domains, the differences between scientists and artists when it comes to emotion, and the importance of reflective self-criticism.

Weisberg, Robert W. (1996)
Creativity. Beyond the Myth of Genius
This book explores the muses providing inspiration according to Greek mythology, Columbus discovering what was already there, the importance of finding problems and of divergent/convergent and productive/reproductive thinking in the problem-solving process, the relative nature of genius (Gregor Mendel), and finally the discovery of our DNA by Watson and Crick.

Books on related topics

Bryson, Bill (2004)
A Short History of Nearly Everything
This book describes the history of science, including the greatest scientists and their inventions. It was used to polish some of the details of scientific discoveries (e.g. how it was not Darwin himself who noticed the small differences between the beaks of the Galapagos finches). Primarily sourced from this book were the invention of the Periodic Table and the very first man-made tools.

Dijksterhuis, Ap (2007)
Het slimme onderbewuste. Denken met gevoel
(Translation: 'The intelligent unconscious. Thinking with feeling.') This book highlights the importance of our unconscious brain in filtering data, making decisions, and feeding our consciousness.

Gladwell Malcom (2011)
Outliers
This book investigates how talent and skill work, more specifically the 10,000-hour rule, which teaches that to become an outlier, practice is more important than talent.

Gombrich, E.H. (1995)
The Story of Art
This book was used to learn more about Renaissance art and in particular about the works of Da Vinci and Michelangelo.

Isaacson, Walter (2011)
Steve Jobs
This book discusses Jobs' opposite personality traits and how the creative process at Apple and Pixar worked.

Documentaries

BBC/Horizon (2013)
The Creative Brain; How Insights Work
This documentary explores the neuroscience of creativity. More specifically, how insights happen in the brain, how a low level of white matter induces creativity, and the importance of unusual experiences and mind-wandering.

Berlinger, Joe (2012)
Under African Skies
This documentary shows how Paul Simon's album Graceland came into being.

Harlan, Jan (2001)
Stanley Kubrick: A life in pictures
This documentary discusses the life and works of Stanley Kubrick.

Wetzel, Gereon (2011)
El Bulli: Cooking in Progress
This documentary shows how chef Ferran Adrià and his team at restaurant El Bulli work.

Pangolin Pictures (2010)
Jaws: The Inside Story
This documentary describes in great detail the many difficulties that made Jaws one of the hardest productions Steven Spielberg ever experienced.

General source

Wikipedia (English)

In most cases, Wikipedia has been used as a secondary source, to have certain findings confirmed or learn more about a topic referred to in another source. Some (but not all) of the lemmas used; Andy Warhol, Apollo 13, Avant-garde, David, Dogme 95, dopamine, Fountain, Henry Moore, Michelangelo, Mona Lisa, printing press, Rosalind Franklin, Sydney Opera House, The Physical Impossibility of Death in the Mind of Someone Living, Thomas Edison, and white matter.

More

If you want to learn more about creativity beyond the sources mentioned here, please visit www.defininingcreativity.com, which is a permanent platform for content about creativity.